Praise for Jim Hardy and
The Plane Truth for Golfers Master Class

"Jim Hardy is the most knowledgeable teacher in golf. I say this based on my association with Jim as my friend and golf instructor for nearly 20 years. No other instructor has his understanding of golf swings and what makes them work. I met Jim at Riviera Country Club during the 1983 PGA championship. It was early in the week, and I was hitting the ball poorly. I asked Jim for help, and by the week's end, on a Sunday afternoon, I was standing on the 72nd hole of a major championship tied for the lead. Although I did not win, that week was the beginning of a great journey with this remarkable man. Any golfer, regardless of ability, who has the opportunity to listen and work with Jim will benefit and improve."

—Peter Jacobsen, winner of seven PGA Tour championships
and 2004 U.S. Senior Open

"I was a top 30 PGA Tour player and, like all golfers, I wanted to get better. That effort turned into a nightmare. Within two years, I had practically fallen off the Tour. At my lowest point, I was recommended to Jim Hardy. He convinced me that the instruction I had been pursuing did not match my swing type. I abandoned the harmful instruction and learned what worked for me. Thanks to Jim, since that turnaround, I have become a multiple tournament winner."

—Scott McCarron, winner of three PGA Tour championships

"All my life I have been a great admirer of Ben Hogan and built my swing around his principles. My career had been a constant struggle between success and failure. By the time I met Jim Hardy, the failure was far outweighing the success. Jim explained why my swing was failing. I understood for the first time that there are two sets of fundamentals. We simply eliminated the ones that did not belong in my swing, and within six months I had won a PGA Tour title and 1.4 million dollars."

—Tom Pernice, winner of two PGA Tour championships

"I've been working with Jim Hardy for about 10 years. Every time I get into a slump, and they now are far and few between, I go visit Jim and he always knows what swing part I've got wrong and fixes it. What's amazing is how quickly I get results. I also like the fact that he's never really changed my swing. Instead, he has taught me what works in my swing and what does not. Jim's the greatest, and I'm so pleased that he is sharing his secrets with golfers in *The Plane Truth for Golfers*."

—Duffy Waldorf, winner of four PGA Tour championships

"In my over 50 years, from a young girl to present, I have known, read about, or worked with nearly every great instructor in the game. In my book, Jim Hardy is at the top. His information is the best. His presentation is logical and unique. Jim is a risk taker and a teacher who loves to probe for new ideas. He has discovered, through original thought, new information that will help every golfer. I have seen it at work, and the results are amazing, as you will find out when reading *The Plane Truth for Golfers*."

—Carol Mann, winner of the U.S. Women's Open Championship

"Jim Hardy is the best communicator I have ever heard on the lesson tee, and I believe he is about to be recognized as one of the top three or four instructors in golf. He is that good."

—Jim Achenbach, Golfweek *magazine senior writer and winner of the World Golf Writers' Championship*

"Our excerpt of *The Plane Truth for Golfers* by Jim Hardy in the May 2005 issue was unprecedented. Unprecedented both in terms of scale—the article ran 16 full pages—and in the reaction it has generated among readers. We've received more e-mails about the article than any other instruction feature in recent *Golf Digest* history."

—Scott Smith, Golf Digest

"Finally there's a book that clarifies the fundamentals of golf based on the swing shape that's right for you. Hardy has the best golf mind I've ever been around. He has made golf easier to teach and learn. You know exactly what to work on and what to avoid. I have seen it with my own eyes. Using his approach, my students improve at a faster rate. Their swing thoughts are simpler so they can get beyond swing mechanics and get on with playing the game. They are hitting longer and straighter shots even under pressure. The results are amazing and fast. Read this book and have fun playing golf your way."

—*Mike LaBauve, voted by* Golf Magazine *and* Golf Digest *as one of America's top teachers*

"Jim Hardy is on most short lists of great golf instructors, and any such roster that does not include his name is incomplete. Few people wear as many hats in the golf industry, and none wear them as well."

—*Doug Pike,* Houston Chronicle

"Golfers usually turn to club pros when they need help with their swing, but where do the pros go when they need help in teaching? In growing numbers, they are sitting at the feet of Jim Hardy, a former PGA Tour pro whose 'plane and simple' theory might provide the answer to why most golfers struggle to improve."

—*John Davis,* The Arizona Republic

"Look up the definition of a thinking man's PGA Professional in a dictionary and you might see a picture of Jim Hardy."

—*Steve Pike, PGA.com senior writer*

"The chapters are very logical. Hardy takes a tested, pragmatic view at what he's tried in the past and how other golfers have reacted to his concepts. Being a good teacher, he offers a summary and review after each topic."

—*Robert Gable,* Pinehurst Magazine

"(Jim Hardy) is the reason I'm in golf today. He was the pro at Exmoor Country Club when I was coming up. He's the Einstein of golf instruction."

—*Jim Murphy, PGA golf professional*

"I want to thank you for not only enlightening me but helping me to become a significantly better teacher by finally putting the golf swing and its mechanics in a proper order. The last two days at your seminar cleared things up so much for me in both my teaching and playing that I have been nominated as a top 100 teacher by *Golf Digest* and recognized as a top teacher in the Northeast. I also enjoy getting to the practice range again and working on my own game."

—*Mike Stubblefield, PGA golf professional, Elmwood Country Club*

"*The Plane Truth for Golfers* by Jim Hardy is the best instruction book I have ever read—bar none."

—*golfblogger.com*

"Owning over 200 golf-related books, I can say that this is probably the most valuable one I've read to date. I strongly recommend this book to any serious golfer."

—*Paul Sherrington, Marietta, Georgia*

"Jim Hardy has written a true masterpiece of golf instruction."

—*deeprough.com*

"After spending large amounts of money on golf training aids and lessons with no remarkable improvement, I purchased *The Plane Truth for Golfers* as a last-ditch effort. No one ever explained golf like Jim Hardy. I couldn't believe it was that simple. I could easily see why I was inconsistent and that applying information from one swing approach doesn't work in the other swing approach. Thank you Jim Hardy for being the best golf teacher I have ever encountered."

—*Keith Benline, San Diego, California*

The Plane Truth for Golfers

MASTER CLASS

The Plane Truth for Golfers

MASTER CLASS

Advanced Lessons for Improving Swing Technique and
Ball Control for the One-Plane and Two-Plane Swings

JIM HARDY

WITH JOHN ANDRISANI

New York Chicago San Francisco Lisbon London Madrid Mexico City
Milan New Delhi San Juan Seoul Singapore Sydney Toronto

Library of Congress Cataloging-in-Publication Data

Hardy, Jim.
    The plane truth for golfers master class: advanced lessons for improving swing
technique and ball control for the one-plane and two-plane swings / by Jim Hardy
with John Andrisani.
      p. cm.
    ISBN 0-07-148240-7 (alk. paper)
    1. Swing (Golf)—Handbooks, manuals, etc.   I. Andrisani, John.   II. Title.

GV979.S9H293   2007
796.352'3—dc22   2006027124

1 2 3 4 5 6 7 8 9 10 11 12 13 14 15 DOC/DOC 0 9 8 7

ISBN-13: 978-0-07-148240-0
ISBN-10:   0-07-148240-7

Interior design by Nick Panos
Interior photographs by Yasuhiro Tanabe

McGraw-Hill books are available at special quantity discounts to use as premiums
and sales promotions, or for use in corporate training programs. For more information,
please write to the Director of Special Sales, Professional Publishing, McGraw-Hill, Two
Penn Plaza, New York, NY 10121-2298. Or contact your local bookstore.

This book is printed on acid-free paper.

I dedicate this second instructional book to John Jacobs,
who first taught me the logical steps to diagnosis, explanation, and correction;
to the multitude of teachers, amateur golfers, and professional golfers around
the world who believe in my ideas and have encouraged me to further
expand upon them; and to Him in His Matchless Grace.

Contents

Foreword

I couldn't be happier or more excited with the success of Jim Hardy's *The Plane Truth for Golfers* and its impact on golfers around the world. I've been lucky enough to gain Jim's knowledge firsthand these past 20 years, and it's not surprising that *The Plane Truth for Golfers* is now distributed in many languages. That tells me two things: The popularity of golf is booming worldwide, and golfers of all levels are very interested in Jim's theories.

In *The Plane Truth for Golfers*, Jim set out the science that there is not one universal set of swing fundamentals in golf, but there are two very different sets of swing fundamentals: one set for a one-plane swing and another for the two-plane swing. He detailed the differences between the two swing types and instructed the golfer on what to do to improve his or her swing. Learning these differences and understanding what to do is essential to your development as a player. The information you'll find in *The Plane Truth for Golfers Master Class* will take you a few steps further in understanding this breakthrough information. In this second book, Jim will teach you *how* to do through actual lessons. All you need to do is identify the problem areas of your swing and find the lessons appropriate to your game. Jim helps you find your lessons through ball flight descriptions, swing shape, and lots of photographs that illustrate swing mistakes and their corrections. You will understand if you are a one- or two-planer and will identify your own swing shape needs and ball flight errors. From taking hundreds of lessons from Jim, I know that after studying your lessons you will understand your mistakes, how to correct them, and what the corrections should feel like. You will now know how to implement the correct fundamentals and will be on your way to "owning" your swing.

I can't stress enough how important it is, while attempting to make a swing change, to exaggerate the motion Jim asks of you. Only through this exaggeration can you truly make the necessary changes. As silly as these radical moves may feel or look, they help to quicken the improvement process. Jim works with me during each and every session, as he does with all of his PGA Tour and Champions Tour students, on making a change by first feeling what an exaggerated mistake feels like. We then make the exaggerated correct move, and from there we can find and feel our way to where we need to be. It is through this method that Jim succeeds in translating information into feel, which is the critical link to "taking it to the course." You will find his "Fact Versus Feel" section in every lesson in this book to be essential.

Jim Hardy continues to impress and amaze me with his passion for the game, his drive to continue to learn, and his ability to communicate his ideas to his pupils. I look forward to all of our continuing education and tutelage in Jim Hardy's Master Class!

—Peter Jacobsen
2004 U.S. Senior Open Champion

Acknowledgments

The success of my first golf book, *The Plane Truth for Golfers*, paved the way for this new instructional text, again published by McGraw-Hill, ushered in through this renowned house's senior editor Mark Weinstein, whom I thank for his patience and professionalism.

I'm also grateful to literary agent Farley Chase of the Waxman Agency in New York City and attorney Mark Crosby for their able work.

I thank John Andrisani, my collaborator and former senior instruction editor of *Golf Magazine*, for his creative input and writing and organizational skills.

Thanks also go out to photographer Yasuhiro Tanabe for helping to visually relay my instructional messages.

My longtime professional students and friends Peter Jacobsen, Tom Pernice Jr., Duffy Waldorf, Scott McCarron, Olin Browne, and Don Pooley also deserve a great deal of credit, because in working with them I was able to crystallize my theories on the one-plane and two-plane swings and share these secrets with you in the form of unique golf lessons.

Last, I would be remiss to leave out a roster of fellow golf professionals and serious amateur golfers who have attended my two-day seminars throughout the years. It is in working with these dedicated students of the game under an intense learning environment that I have been forced to constantly improve and update my verbal, visual, and kinesthetic communication skills. I also owe

Acknowledgments

a great deal to the professionals who teach in these seminars with me: Mike and Sandy LaBauve, Paul Gorman, Chris O'Connell, E. J. Pfister, Marty Fleckman, Carol Mann, Wally Hynes, and Roger Gunn—who, for years, I've depended on for feedback on what started out to be the one-plane/two-plane theory and is now what my followers believe is the best method for teaching and learning golf.

Introduction

There have been few things in my life that have provided me with the sense of accomplishment I experienced after my first golf instruction book, *The Plane Truth for Golfers*, became such a big hit as a top-selling golf book that appeared on several bestseller lists within the golf category. In fact, it's still selling phenomenally well to the golfing public and also being positively received by the teaching world.

I won't say much more about my first book right now, since I will review segments of it in Chapter 1. I do this for the benefit of those golfers who have not yet read *The Plane Truth for Golfers* but need to know the basic differences between the one-plane and two-plane swings and how to choose the best technique for them.

Golf is a game that most players expect to learn quickly, when in truth the greatest professionals in the world—even present-day wonder Tiger Woods—admit to learning something new nearly every day.

Over time you, like all good players, will develop a versatile repertoire of shots. The thing is, before you can achieve that ambitious goal, you must learn a repeating golf swing—either a one-plane or a two-plane action that becomes so well grooved that during play on the course it is directed to a large degree by the feel rather than the conscious mind. Trust me, this is one secret to success.

Whereas *The Plane Truth for Golfers* laid down the groundwork on *what* to do, *The Plane Truth for Golfers Master Class* provides one- and two-plane golfers with lessons on *how* to improve swing technique and ball control.

In a former life, I played golf for a living on tour, and I have been teaching the game for decades. However, before my first book hit the bookstores and created such a stir, golfers had heard of me either through my course architect work or my longtime teacher-student relationship with Peter Jacobsen, a multiple winner on the PGA Tour, the 2004 U.S. Senior Open winner, and the 2005 Senior Ford TPC champion who, incidentally, is also my golf course design partner.

I'm pleased that my first book let golfers know the reason they were failing to improve at golf was not their fault. It was just that they were confused by misinformation regarding the "basics" or, more specifically, mixing one-plane fundamentals with two-plane fundamentals. Your lesson: *All swings are either one-plane or two-plane actions, and to become good at golf you must work toward being a fundamental purist, only learning and employing those elements relative to your swing type.*

I refer to my first book as a scientific text because it stated a new philosophy on teaching golf and provided golfers with one-plane and two-plane building blocks. In contrast, *The Plane Truth for Golfers Master Class*, a more sophisticated and advanced book, takes swing technique to new heights, focusing on the *art* of the golf swing. This new book describes through words and pictures the ideal movements and positions of each swing type, as well as the common incorrect elements or mistakes of each swing technique, and teaches you how to get on track and become a more consistent player. I'll go into much more detail about the two swing types in this book's introductory chapter, and I will also give you a fuller preview of what to expect from my lessons. But right now let me make one thing clear: Both the one-plane and two-plane swings are good swings, and the ideal goal for each is for you to come as close as possible to matching the general good positions without letting yourself become so technically minded that you tense up physically or become confused mentally.

Since many golfers around the globe communicated to me that they wanted more information on how to mold a one- or two-plane swing action, I'm going to answer this calling in the book you are about to read.

I cannot promise that by reading *The Plane Truth for Golfers Master Class* you will evolve into as good a one-plane swinger as Michelle Wie or Peter Jacobsen, or as good a two-plane swinger as David Toms, Tom Watson, or Karrie Webb. However, I will guarantee this: If you follow the lessons I conduct in this book, you will develop a technically sound one- or two-plane swing that flows and operates so efficiently that when you hit shots you will experience the sensation of effortlessness—a sure sign that the body, arms, and club are all working in a coordinated fashion.

In my telling you this, please do not get the impression that you will play good golf all of the time. The game of golf can never be perfected. Nevertheless, in due time, via my lessons, you will be provided with the right technical information so that during those times when you do go off your game and your swing stops working well, you will know how to correct your faults and return to good form.

I believe wholeheartedly that *The Plane Truth for Golfers Master Class* is unique because rather than offer false promises it addresses the golfer's problems straight on and teaches you the keys to developing as good a swing as is physically possible to employ. This is done by developing correct one- or two-plane positions and learning the art of managing your faults. Furthermore, this book will create a special kind of optimism in the heads of golfers because they will not only know what to work on to improve, but also how to do it.

I consider myself a low-key man. Consequently, I'm not big on standing on a pedestal, patting my chest, and saying that my method has the "it" quality. However, I'm proud to say that, in addition to receiving positive reactions from amateurs who said my one- and two-plane philosophies turned their games around, I've received accolades from golf instructors who, after attending Plane Truth clinics I conducted across the country, have admitted to me that they were wrong about the way they were teaching golf. What impressed me more is hearing that after adopting my methods for teaching the one-plane and two-plane swings, they continue to see incredible results in their students. I make these teachers feel a whole lot better when I open up and admit that I also once believed in the one set of evergreen fundamentals and, as a result, often harmed as many golfers as I helped.

It was, of course, important for me to discover that all swings are either one-plane or two-plane actions. Furthermore, I found that the more athletic and flexible the student is, the more he or she is suited to the one-plane swing, while the less athletic student is often better suited to the two-plane action.

Having said this, more than distinguishing between two swings, the biggest breakthrough for me came when I figured out that the one-plane swinger needs to set up differently and also work the body, arms, and club much differently on the backswing and downswing than the two-plane swinger. Moreover, it became clear that the only true shortcut for learning a new swing, whether it be a one-plane or two-plane action, is to work on various drills and "feels" during practice.

That said, let's go to the practice tee, where I'll conduct today's introductory preview lesson.

The Plane Truth for Golfers

MASTER CLASS

Laying the Groundwork

The driving force behind writing *The Plane Truth for Golfers Master Class*, as a follow-up to *The Plane Truth for Golfers*, published in 2005, was very similar to what got me passionately reinvolved in teaching golf back in 1994, following a hiatus of nearly 12 years. That impetus was the excitement of discovering that there are indeed two different types of swings, the one-plane and two-plane actions, and the positive reactions I received from amateur students and also tour professionals, most notably PGA Tour and Champions Tour player Peter Jacobsen, whom I helped become a one-plane swinger.

If you have read my first book, you now know what type of swing suits you best, and you know that one secret to success is never letting a two-plane setup or swing fundamental slip into your one-plane method or vice versa.

Just in case you have not read *The Plane Truth for Golfers*, at the end of this chapter I will again lay down the criteria for helping you choose the swing that will work best for you, or for your students if you are an instructor searching for a proven methodology. As a preview of what's to come, let me provide you with some vital one- and two-plane descriptions.

In order to best understand the differences between the two types of technique, you must first appreciate that the one-plane golfer bends over quite a bit at address and plays out of a wide stance, while the two-plane golfer stands quite erect and plays out of a narrow stance.

Photos 1.1–1.2 One-plane address

Photos 1.3–1.4 Two-plane address

The second major defining element of the two techniques involves the relationship between the arm-swing and the body-turn. The arms swing upward from address onto either somewhat the same plane the body turns on (a one-plane swing) or onto a different plane than the body turns on (a two-plane swing). Described another way: The one-plane swinger swings the arms and club around the body while allowing the body to turn as fully and as hard as is comfortably possible; the two-plane swinger keeps the swinging arms and club up and down in front of the body while the body turns in time with the arm-swing.

Speaking as a veteran teacher, it was very satisfying to feel I had made a true breakthrough in discovering that there are, indeed, two types of swings, each dictated by a separate set of fundamentals; this was a breakthrough so revolutionary it was bound to trigger a paradigm shift in the way the game of golf should be taught. Yet it was even more satisfying to know that I had, in fact, solved the mystery of how to sort out all the information on the golf swing so that now, golfers could decide what information fit their swing. This is verified by the e-mails, letters, and telephone calls I received from amateur and professional golfers who purchased *The Plane Truth for Golfers*, read the 16-page excerpt that appeared in *Golf Digest* magazine, or watched the clinics I gave on the Golf Channel's *Academy Live* segment.

Photo 1.5 One-plane top of backswing

Photo 1.6 Two-plane top of backswing

I invite you to read a sampling of the over 3,000 responses I have received from golfers who purchased *The Plane Truth for Golfers*, read the *Golf Digest* excerpt, and saw my appearances on the Golf Channel. Reading these comments will make you more confident about my teaching method, give you insights into the one- and two-plane swings, and provide you with a foundation for the more detailed technical information that is explained in this book's upcoming chapters.

Reactions to *The Plane Truth for Golfers*

"As a PGA member and professional golf instructor, I am sending along this note of thanks for your most recent book, *The Plane Truth for Golfers*. I have worked with the game's top teachers, most notably Hank Haney, Tiger Woods's present coach, and read his books as well as those by such legendary professionals as Ben Hogan and Jack Nicklaus. However, I have never read golf instruction written with the clarity and correctness for which your book was written."

—Don Sargent Jr. (Oakmont, Pennsylvania)

"*The Plane Truth for Golfers* is the best golf book I have ever read. It is extremely instructive, and so clear that it takes away the confusion that has surrounded this game for too, too long."

—Paolo Polledri (San Francisco, California)

"*The Plane Truth for Golfers* is the best golf instructional book I have ever read. I say that because it opened my eyes to a new way of looking at the golf swing. I have never seen such a clear explanation of what role each part of the body plays in the backswing and downswing. I just wish I had this information at my disposal seven years ago when I began playing golf. I know if I did, I would never have struggled so."

—Ashish Misra (India)

Reactions to *Golf Digest*'s Feature Story on *The Plane Truth for Golfers*

"I wish I could invite Jim Hardy to dinner. The article in your magazine encouraged me to continue playing with my one-plane swing and to stop thinking about quitting golf. Teachers had always discouraged me from swinging my way. Not Jim Hardy. His article helped me discard the two-plane elements in my one-plane swing and hit the ball so solidly it sounded like a bullet coming off the clubface."

—Dan Mitchell (Lewisbury, Pennsylvania)

"I'm somewhat flexible and have more of a bulky build, so I tried Jim Hardy's one-plane swing explained very clearly in your magazine's excerpt of *The Plane Truth for Golfers*. In this article was the best golf instruction I have ever received. I now hit the ball much longer and straighter, and it's so easy."

—Ken Gaitan (Austin, Texas)

"After reading Jim Hardy's instructional article that appeared in your publication and was based on the book *The Plane Truth for Golfers*, a light bulb went off in my head. Hardy convinced me to be a one-plane swinger and initiate the downswing with a bump of the hips. Now I can hit the ball as long as 300 yards off the tee."

—Robert Lusetich (Australia)

Reactions to the Golf Channel's Segment on *The Plane Truth for Golfers*

"The 'Academy Live' segment, in which Jim Hardy and student Peter Jacobsen explained the Plane Truth philosophy, was the most enlightening one hour of television I have ever witnessed. I could not wait to get to the golf course and see what technique, one- or two-plane, yielded the best results."

—Jim Mulcahy (Willow Springs, Illinois)

"Your recent segment with Jim Hardy and Peter Jacobsen, discussing the one-plane versus two-plane swing, was the best golf lesson I've ever received. It helped simplify things so much that I solidified my own technique and am now able to hit the ball a whole lot better."

—David Briggs (Hanford, California)

"When I saw Mr. Hardy and Mr. Jacobsen on 'Academy Live,' I realized that I was a natural one-planer who was wrongly having to become a two-planer. To shorten a long story, I tried bending over more at address, like Jake, and I returned to my old form."

—Robert Vowell (Picayune, Mississippi)

Aside from the obvious sense of accomplishment I felt after reading what amateurs and professionals had to say about my first book, I knew that there was more work to do. In short, I needed to write a second book that would take golfers like you further along the road to improvement.

The Plane Truth for Golfers was a scientific instructional text, providing golfers with a brand-new vocabulary of fundamentals, and telling them *what to do* when employing either a one- or two-plane swing. This new second book, *The Plane Truth for Golfers Master Class*, is a *how-to* book that focuses on the *art* of technique and provides golfers with lessons for improving their swing technique and ball control for the one-plane and two-plane swings. Whereas the first book was more educational, simply because it laid out two proven sets of fundamentals, this new hard-hitting text is more sophisticated in that it takes golfers further along the learning curve by teaching them how to start from scratch and build a technically correct one- or two-plane swing or revamp an old faulty swing by implementing the right body-arm-club elements into their existing action. This time, in putting pen to paper, I also relied on teacher-student case studies, most involving myself and a tour professional, so that golfers like you will be able to improve using the following methods:

- Learning the correct address, backswing, and downswing elements of the one-plane and two-plane setup and swing
- Receiving lessons on identifying faults
- Understanding ball flight patterns that can be traced to each of the faulty positions cited so that you can pinpoint your address or swing problem
- Being given specific solutions to your problems
- Learning the facts about fixing faults in your one-plane or two-plane technique through feel (sometimes even getting the sense that you are in the wrong position when actually you are helping yourself establish the right position)

When thinking out the structure of this new book, I purposely chose a "voice" that would allow you, the golfer-reader, to feel as if I were right next to you on the driving range conducting a private lesson. This is most obvious when I am getting a point across about learning what to feel in order to correct a fault and get the fundamental fact right. Let me explain to you what I mean by citing an anecdotal example:

Fact: In teaching Peter Jacobsen (or any other one-plane swinger), I want the arms to stay "connected" during the downswing as the arms swing around the chest (rather than move away from the chest) and the torso to turn in order that the club be delivered squarely and solidly into the ball at impact.

Feel: To help Peter learn to employ the correct swing motions, I sometimes have him imagine that at the top of the backswing, a large elastic band is tight around his upper arms (just above the elbows) and chest to keep his upper arms tight to his body so that he cannot move them out from his chest as he turns his torso and swings his arms around his chest to the left.

By using the Fact Versus Feel information provided in my lessons, you, like Peter and my other students, will purify your contaminated golf swing and hit the ball much better. Moreover, with my guidance, by the time you finish reading this book (and, ideally, my first book, if you haven't already), you will be able to categorize all golf information as either one-plane information, two-plane information, or worthless information.

As you'll soon learn, *The Plane Truth for Golfers Master Class* defines each of the two types of swinging actions separately. I suggest that if you are a one-plane swinger, you first read all of the chapters on your type action relative to the address, backswing, and downswing—while, of course, also looking at the accompanying photographs to help you better understand the instruction. Then, if you are curious, read about the two-plane setup and swing, noting varying aspects of that technique, just so you know what not to do and more quickly become a one-plane purist. Two-plane swingers should simply heed the opposite instructions, reading about their technique first and the one-plane action second. That's my suggestion, anyway.

The major focal point of this second book revolves around the golf lessons I give to golfers, starting with descriptions of the ideal movements and positions for each swing. These ideal elements will be separated and identified in two ways: body movements and positions and arm and club movements and positions for the two swing types. Each ideal movement and position will be illustrated by photographs and explained in detail via accompanying text and captions.

The lessons I give assume that you, like most golfers, struggle somewhat in achieving these ideal elements of the golf swing and thus are usually out of position. Chances are, though, that you are not out of position in myriad ways.

Based on my teaching experience, most of the time golfers make only two mistakes relative to the correct position. The mistakes are usually a "yin" or a "yang" or, more simply put, an overexaggeration or an "underexaggeration" of the correct move. Typically, you or other golfers will have gotten into a position or movement that is either too steep or too narrow, too wide or too shallow, too much in-to-out or too much out-to-in relative to the correct position or movement.

In a few instances, there may be only one common mistake, and in a few others there may be more than two common errors. So the next part of the lesson will focus on the common mistakes that are made relative to the correct element and how to identify which mistake you may be making. Photographs will illustrate the mistakes, and again there will be accompanying text explaining the mistake as well as ball flight descriptions (such as pulls or slice shot patterns) to help identify the problem.

Next, while giving lessons to one-plane and two-plane golfers, I'll explain why you and other players make mistakes and then offer corrective instruction on what you must do to achieve the ideal position. I will provide drills to help you practice the instruction. In all cases, the aforementioned Fact Versus Feel segments will give you an exaggerated feel for the correction. Sometimes I'll even include some of the instruction on just the same mistakes I have helped PGA Tour professionals such as student Peter Jacobsen to overcome, and I will report what their feelings were when correcting a mistake.

The next segment of your lesson will involve application—how you can apply the instruction to your game. As a preface to what is needed for you to accomplish your goals, you must first master the recommended course of action in the practice swing. Since the feel of the correction is often exaggerated, the practice swing will also need to be somewhat exaggerated. Making an exaggerated practice swing is, I believe, vital to the amount of time it takes to incorporate the correction. Many of the PGA Tour professionals I teach make exaggerated practice swings just before initiating their one- or two-plane action, even in tournaments.

I have had many a gallery fan recognize me at a tour event and ask why Peter Jacobsen or Olin Browne makes such an outside-in practice swing or why Tom Pernice Jr., another of my pro students, waggles the club so upright during his preswing routine. The reason why for Peter, Olin, Tom, you, or any other golfer is the same. In our practice swings, and even in our actual swings on the driving range, we might actually exaggerate the correction. However, once on the course, whatever exaggeration you had in your swing will naturally be gone when you hit the ball.

The golf course will always tend to make us revert to our old habits. You can exaggerate nearly as much as you like on the course with your practice swing. Because you are on the course, the swing at the ball will not be an exaggeration and will probably turn out to be correct. It may still *feel* like an exaggeration when you hit the ball, but trust me, it won't be. Without this exaggeration, you will not overcome your old tendencies when faced with a target during actual play. For this reason, it is vital to view and rehearse your practice swings in front of a mirror. Look at the position and movement you are trying to achieve relative to your own one- or two-plane swing. Next, slightly exaggerate the position in the mirror. Don't go too far overboard. Just exaggerate slightly past where perfect would be. Also, try to memorize what the feeling of making the move is like. Rehearse over and over until you see what position you are supposed to be in. Once you feel that you have mastered the move, try employing it on the practice range.

Before beginning your new Plane Truth journey, a word of caution is needed. Working on golf swings is a little like steering a boat in high winds and heavy seas. You are constantly moving the tiller one way and then the other in order to maintain a true course. It is the same with golf and for all golfers, even tour players. Anytime you are trying to make a change, one of these things will happen:

- The change will result in permanently allowing you to achieve the ideal position.
- You achieve the ideal position, but over time you revert to the same old bad habits.
- The change will allow you to achieve the ideal position, but then you will overexaggerate a movement or movements of your swing so much that you end up on the other side of your mistake.
- Nothing changes, you simply employ the same old bad habits.

Knowing when to push harder against your mistake and when to back off is the art of becoming a pure one- or two-plane swinger and shot-making virtuoso.

To check your progress and ensure that you are pushing in the right direction, follow the flight of the ball. If the shape and trajectory of your shots are heading toward your ideal pattern, you are improving. If the flight pattern of your shots fails to change, rest assured your swing is not changing for the better. Last, if your ball flight pattern is opposite to your old shot shape, you are probably pushing too hard.

Another good way to check your progress is to have a friend analyze your one- or two-plane swing and tell you if you are in the right or wrong position. However, be careful not to judge by your practice swings since, as I stated previously in this chapter, they are usually more exaggerated than the actions you employ when hitting balls. The secret is to alter your practice swing for more or less exaggeration, depending on what type of shots you hit and how far off the mark you are.

Choosing Your Swing

If you have not read my previous book and have never experimented with these two very different types of swings, you might well be concerned about which method to adopt. "If I make the wrong choice," you might be thinking, "I may end up playing worse than I am right now!"

I would like to banish that concern from your mind immediately. In truth, there is no wrong choice in deciding whether to become a one-plane or two-plane swinger. I feel very confident in stating that if you are a golfer who scores above 80 (and that would include the vast majority of all amateurs), and if you do a reasonably diligent job of learning and applying the techniques of either type of swing, you will see a dramatic improvement in your tee-to-green play.

Note that I said you need only do a reasonable job of applying either set of principles. The truth is, nobody has ever developed a perfect one-plane or two-plane swing. (I do feel that Ben Hogan came as close as any player yet to perfecting, in his case, the one-plane swing action.) There are many outstanding Tour players who are essentially one-plane swingers, who include one or two elements of two-plane actions in their swings, and vice versa. The principles we will be discussing in this Master Class book are the ideals for you to work on. If you can come close to developing either set of swing principles perfectly, believe me, you will become a better striker of the ball than you have ever imagined.

Peter Jacobsen and Don Pooley are the best models of PGA Tour players who successfully changed from one of the two methods to the other in midcareer. (In both cases, it was from the two-plane swing to the one-plane swing.) I changed Don from two-plane swinger to one-plane swinger in 2005 after lower back and left shoulder injuries had severely limited his two-plane playing ability. We tried to make the change over a two-month period. After the two months were up, our plan was to evaluate Don's ability to compete at the high level needed on the Champions Tour as a one-planer. If we felt that he could not handle the change, we were going to try to find a way he could play a limited schedule around his physical problems with his two-plane swing. When we got together at the end of the two months, before I could say a word, Don said, "I'm never going back. I'm hitting the ball wonderful and experiencing no pain. I'm going with it." In short, Don went with the change and has never looked back.

Don's record on the Champions the past two years is remarkable and is a tribute to his determination to learn a new and different swing at an age of over 50 and succeed with it at the highest levels.

I had worked with Peter as far back as 1983. At that time, I had not fully defined and organized my thinking about the golf swing into the one-plane and two-plane concepts. Nevertheless, I did begin working informally with Peter at the 1983 PGA Championship, which was contested at Riviera Country Club in Los Angeles, California. When I say we worked informally, what I really mean is, I was talking with Peter on the practice range about his two-plane swing problems. Although Peter had not been striking the ball particularly well, I did not want to shove my advice down his throat, right there on the eve of a major championship. I felt that delving into the mechanics of his swing right before the tournament would hurt his chances of playing well. You must realize, even if a talented Tour player like Peter had been struggling a bit, you never could tell which week he would get into a good rhythm with the swing he had and get hot with the putter at the same time. I didn't want to do or say anything that might prevent Peter from having one of those "on" weeks.

But Peter is a curious person, a real student of the golf swing, and he is also by nature a risk-taker. So he decided that he was going to play that week with some of the new swing thoughts I had offered relating to his two-plane swing. Well, it turned out that Peter had a tremendous week. He was in close contention down the stretch and wound up finishing third behind winner Hal Sutton and runner-up Jack Nicklaus.

Peter had moderate success over the next eight or nine years, but I'm sure not as much as he would have liked and not nearly as much as I thought he was capable of. In 1993, Peter, due to back injuries and a television offer he couldn't refuse, became a part-time player, part-time broadcaster, thinking he might phase out his playing career. Instead, he found that broadcasting rekindled his appetite to compete and compete well. Late that next year, Peter and I talked about his playing full-time again.

By that time, I had honed my knowledge of the one- and two-plane swings. Peter had always been in the two-plane category, albeit a two-plane swing that was hurting his back. He was keenly interested, as was I, in seeing if he could make the change from two-plane to one-plane and return back to the Tour full-time. So we started working on it intensively and have done so ever since. The record book speaks for itself. Peter had the best year of his career in 1995, winning two tournaments at age 41. In 2003, at age 49, Peter won the Hartford Open. The following year, in his first try as a senior, Peter took the U.S. Senior Open title, and in the next, the Senior Players Championship—two majors. I am sure he will be a dominant force on the Champions Tour for as long as he has his competitive fire for the game of golf.

The biggest challenge for you, like both Peter and Don, is to decide which swing type works best for you and stick with it. If you have been playing for some time but do not have a clear notion of what to do to hit the ball both powerfully and straight, you need to make a choice, too. Your swing development will come easier to you if you choose the swing that better suits your overall physical condition, strength, and flexibility. To that end, I want you to take a simple test that might help you decide whether to go with the one-plane or two-plane swing, then I will explain why.

Stand facing a wall, with the tips of your toes approximately 12 inches away from it. Assume a stance that is fairly wide, so that the insides of your heels are the width of the outside of your shoulders. Flex your knees slightly, as you would when taking your address position. Instead of letting your arms hang down, hold a club across your shoulders on the front of your chest. Finally, lean your head and upper body forward until the top of your forehead is touching the wall. Your spine will thus be tilted forward at approximately a 35-degree angle.

13

With the exception of the fact that your arms are holding the club across your shoulders, your posture, as you will see, is that of a one-plane golfer at address. It is important that you take the test from this starting position.

From here, simply turn your shoulders as fully to your right as you are able, just as you would in the backswing for a drive. Make sure that you turn your chest and shoulders and also allow the lower half of your body to turn. Do not restrict your hip turn. Hold that position. Now see where the end of the club shaft is pointing. If the shaft is perfectly perpendicular to the wall, it means you have turned your shoulders 90 degrees.

If the shaft points slightly right of perpendicular to the wall, it means you turned your shoulders more than 90 degrees. If the shaft points to the left of perpendicular to the wall, you've turned your shoulders less than 90 degrees.

Photo 1.7 One-plane flexibility test: starting position

Photo 1.8 One-plane flexibility test: ending position

My basic recommendation that comes from this exercise is this: If you can turn your shoulders and upper body fairly close to 90 degrees (at least to the 75-degree range), the chances are very good that you are capable of maximizing your abilities by using the one-plane swing. A large shoulder turn does not mean you must use the one-plane swing, it simply indicates you are capable of applying it well. If, on the other hand, you determine that your shoulder turn is well short of 90 degrees (say, less than 75 degrees), you may not be allowing your hips and lower body to turn far enough to reach 75 degrees. Try the test again, this time allowing the lower body to turn. If you are still short of 75 degrees, it indicates a lack of flexibility that will make it more difficult for you to develop power with the one-plane swing. Therefore your turn suggests, again not definitively, that you may perform better with the two-plane swing. Let me explain why.

Because the one-plane swing emphasizes the arms swinging and the body turning in somewhat the same plane, timing and tempo are not critical to a consistently repeatable swing. However, the player must be able to turn his or her torso fully and vigorously both on the backswing and on the downswing for the one-plane swing to be very powerful. The two-plane swing, in contrast, relies on a relatively horizontal turn of the shoulders, combined with an active upward-and-downward chopping motion of the arms during the backswing and downswing. Because these horizontal and vertical motions must be blended together, the two-plane swing relies more on perfect timing than does the one-plane swing. It is for this reason that I believe it is harder to develop consistency with the two-plane swing. However, consistency can obviously be accomplished: witness the likes of two-plane swingers Jack Nicklaus, Tom Watson, Davis Love, Karrie Webb, and David Toms.

One advantage of the two-plane swing is that this upward-and-downward, karate chop movement of the arms is the source of tremendous additional power. That is why the player who cannot make a full body turn on the backswing will find that with the one-plane swing, he or she will become more consistent, but may not be able to hit the ball with a great deal of power. If that is the case, the player will find that he or she can generate significantly more clubhead speed with the two-plane action. And the distance that this type of player can gain with the two-plane swing may make it worth his or her while to use the two-plane, even at the loss of some consistency in the swing.

I think it's important to add that this measurement of your shoulder turn is just a guideline. It is not a complete measurement of your ability to generate power. Say, for example, a player can only muster a 70-degree shoulder turn. However, he stands over six feet tall, weighs 220 pounds, and works out regularly using weights and is quite strong in the upper body. I would say that this player can definitely generate plenty of speed and power with a one-plane swing and should not rule it out at all. On the other hand, if a senior player can generate no more than 60 degrees of shoulder turn, chances are he will want all the help he can get in generating clubhead speed. Therefore, although it is again not a must, the two-plane swing would seem to be a better fit.

If you currently do not generate a full shoulder turn but would like to develop the one-plane swing, some time spent in the gym using equipment that strengthens your core muscles will be very wisely spent. You see, when we talk about making a shoulder turn, we are really talking about turning your entire upper torso while allowing your lower body to turn. The stronger and better toned your core muscles, the more fully you will be able to turn your upper torso. There are a number of weight machines in almost all health clubs that work the core; especially good are those that require you to twist your abdomen in either direction. Even if you don't go to the gym, doing a couple of sets of sit-ups or crunches daily will make a big difference. Put in this effort for a few weeks, then test your turn again. You may well find that it has increased, and with it your confidence in implementing the one-plane swing.

I'd like to close this chapter by reiterating a couple of points I made in my first book, *The Plane Truth for Golfers*.

First, in choosing between the one-plane and two-plane swings, you must also address your hand-eye coordination, flexibility, and athletic ability. Specifically, if you are flexible; strong in the chest, abdominal, back, and shoulder muscles; and aggressive too, the one-plane swing will probably suit you better. On the other hand, if you lack body or arm strength and are not flexible, the two-plane action is likely to be your best choice of swing.

I believe the best way to help you decide which method best suits you would be to test both swing types. To test the one-plane swing, bend over about 30 to 40 degrees and then swing your arms and club around your chest like a bent-over baseball hitter.

Photo 1.9 One-plane address

Photo 1.10 One-plane midpoint in backswing

Photo 1.11 One-plane top of backswing

Photo 1.12 One-plane midpoint in downswing

Photo 1.13 One-plane just past impact

Photo 1.14 One-plane follow-through

Then, to test the two-plane swing, stand erect and turn your entire torso, hips, and shoulders to the right (if you are right-handed). At the same time swing your arms and club up and over your right shoulder. Then turn your torso the other way and, at the same time, swing your arms and club down to the ground and then up over your left shoulder as you continue to turn to face the target.

After making practice swings, try hitting balls using both swing methods. One way will feel more natural to you and will hit the ball better than the other. If one feels better and the other hits better, I'd go with the one that hits best. In any case, pick the one that suits you best. Almost all golf swings contain many elements of both swing types. It's why golfers don't play better. So it doesn't make much difference which you choose.

If you implement either swing well, I am completely confident that you will end up hitting the ball better. That's because both methods will help you to apply the energy in your swing with maximum efficiency. By this I mean that you will learn to deliver the center of the clubface so that it meets the back of the ball while it is traveling levelly. If you learn to do this, you will be surprised

Photo 1.15 Two-plane address

Photo 1.16 Two-plane midpoint in backswing

Photo 1.17 Two-plane top of backswing

Photo 1.18 Two-plane midpoint in downswing

Photo 1.19 Two-plane just prior to impact

Photo 1.20 Two-plane follow-through

at how much distance you can gain, even with a relatively slow swing speed. And I might add, proper application of either the one-plane or two-plane swing will also add clubhead speed to your swing, because you are making the clubhead travel through its backswing and downswing arcs with little or no wasted motion. So in terms of distance, you really win two ways. Having said this, all things considered for average players, the one-plane swing is likely to yield more accuracy, while the two-plane swing can provide you with the potential to generate added power.

Now that I have given you some factors to consider in choosing your swing type, it's time to begin a series of Master Class lessons on the ins and outs of the one-plane and two-plane swings.

The One-Plane Address

If you have decided to develop a one-plane golf swing, you must start by adopting a setup that is conducive to this type of swinging action. If you have read other golf instruction books and/or have taken lessons in the past, you will notice that there are some elements of the one-plane setup that are different from what you are accustomed to. However, the sooner you have an intellectual understanding concerning the fundamental facts of the ideal one-plane starting position, the sooner you'll correct the common faults that I'll address in this chapter and also learn to feel more comfortable over the ball.

Model One-Plane Address Positions
Stance: Wider Is Better

For the one-plane swing, you should assume a stance that is slightly wider than the norm. This means that with a driver, the distance between the insides of your heels should be approximately as wide as the shirt seams at the outside of your shoulders.

This relatively wide stance gives you the solid base that you will need to support the aggressive rotation of the entire trunk and to support the resulting wider and somewhat flatter swing arc that is the hallmark, if you will, of the one-plane swing. Of course, as you work your way down through the shorter clubs in the bag, your stance will gradually narrow, but it should remain relatively wide

Photo 2.1 One-plane correct stance

on all full shots. For a full pitching wedge, then, the insides of your heels should still be about 12 inches apart.

In terms of body alignment, the one-plane golfer should basically be square to the target line for all normal full shots. That is, lines drawn across your toes, knees, hips, and shoulders should all point very close to parallel to your target line. Although your right hand (for a right-handed player) is below your left hand on the grip, I want your shoulders as level as you can achieve while keeping them square. You can accomplish this by not allowing your hands much forward of the center of your body at address. More on the club position in a moment.

One other point regarding the one-plane stance: You should point your left or front toe out somewhat, so that it is at least 30 degrees outward from being perpendicular to the target line. This opening of the left foot will automatically allow your hips and upper torso to fully turn through during the downswing and follow-through.

Your weight distribution should be very close to even between the feet, or slightly favoring your left (forward) foot for all full shots. For the one-plane golfer, the weight will also be just a bit more toward the balls of the feet rather than on the heels.

Posture: Bend Into the Zone

The most prominent feature of the one-plane player's setup is a more pronounced forward bending of the upper body. You should bend forward so that your spine is at an angle that's 30 to 45 degrees down from vertical. This is at least 10 degrees more bend than you may be accustomed to.

There's a good reason for this additional forward bend. You see, in the one-plane swing, both the arms and the shoulders will move along a single plane line, on both the back and forward swings. The shoulder turn must be more

Photo 2.2 One-plane address: first test

upright for the one-plane swinger than for the two-planer, who will turn the shoulders on a flatter plane, while swinging the arms up and down along a much steeper plane. And in order for the one-plane player to employ this more upright shoulder turn, while keeping that shoulder turn perpendicular to the spine, it stands to reason that he or she must bend forward significantly more at address. A note of caution here: When you bend forward, make sure you bend your entire torso forward from the hips, not from the waist. Bending from the hips allows you to keep your back straight, whereas bending from the waist will cause you to simply slump your shoulders forward, as opposed to bending the entire torso at a uniform angle.

Here are two checkpoints to make sure you've bent forward sufficiently: First, have a friend dangle a yardstick downward, with the top of the yardstick touching the front of one shoulder. The dangling end of the yardstick should be pointing at least an inch or two in front of the tips of your shoes.

Photo 2.3 One-plane address: second test

A second test is to see if your forward bend puts you in the "zone," which I described in *The Plane Truth for Golfers*. This zone is an imaginary area that runs on the ground from where the golf ball is sitting at address to a point 48 inches to the outside of or beyond the ball. While still in your address position, have your friend place the yardstick down across the top of one shoulder so that the yardstick is at a perfect right angle to your spine. Where does the yardstick point?

If it points anywhere in the middle of the area described, it means you are sufficiently bent forward. If, however, the yardstick points to the outside edge of the zone, or if it points outside the zone (or more than 48 inches beyond the ball), you'll know you're not bending forward enough. In the rare cases where the yardstick points straight at the ball or inside the ball, this means you have bent forward too much. As a general rule, the taller the golfer the more bend is required. Also the shorter the club, the more you must bend.

A couple of additional points regarding your posture: When you have bent forward sufficiently, your arms should be hanging so that your hands are directly underneath your chin. There should be no sensation of reaching toward the ball. Also, if you were observing the posture from a face-on angle, your spine should have no side bend (tilt) and should appear to be perfectly straight, neither tilting toward the target nor away from it. (This, too, is a slight variation from setup advice you may have heard in the past.) Finally, as mentioned earlier, when looking from a face-on view, your hands should be just a touch ahead of the center of your body: essentially, opposite the left seam of the zipper sewed into a man's trousers. This means that, depending on what club you are hitting, your hands will be about even with, slightly behind, or slightly ahead of the ball's position (which we will discuss shortly). This positioning of the hands, too, represents a variation from what you may be accustomed to.

Grip: Neutral to Fairly Strong Is Preferable

I do not believe it is important whether you choose to grip the club using an overlap grip, which was popularized by Harry Vardon and is used by the majority of professional golfers, or the interlock grip employed by Jack Nicklaus. Both of these grips are described in *The Plane Truth for Golfers* and, if you have played and studied the game a bit, I'm sure you are already familiar with them. Whichever style you choose, I believe it is important for you, as a one-plane golfer, to place your hands in a neutral to fairly strong position on the handle. This means that as you look down at address, you should see at least two knuckles of your left hand (neutral position) but no more than three knuckles of that hand (strong position).

When we get into the fine points of the one-plane swing in Chapters 3 and 4, I'll explain why I believe a one-plane golfer can play with a slightly closed clubface.

Ball Position: Check It Two Ways

It is important not only to position the ball correctly in its relation to the feet, but also to be aware of how far away it should be from the feet. In general, the one-plane player should stand slightly farther away from the ball than the two-plane golfer. This should be quite a natural adjustment, since you will be bend-

Photo 2.4 Neutral grip

Photo 2.5 Strong grip

ing forward from the waist more. Therefore, your arms (and the club) also will be a bit farther away from your body than for the two-plane golfer. The length of the club for the shot you are hitting and the amount you need to bend over to be in the zone will determine the overall distance that you stand from the ball.

The position of the ball in relation to the feet, when viewed from a face-on angle, is one point that should not vary whether you employ a one- or two-plane swing. With the driver, the ball should rest on a line drawn to your left heel, or slightly more forward, opposite the left instep. This will allow you to make contact ever so slightly on the upswing, which is desirable with a driver. You will move the ball back in your stance very gradually as the clubs get shorter, until for a full wedge shot, the ball should be just about in the center or just back of center of your stance. This means that with the shorter irons, your hands will be a bit ahead of the clubface so that you deliver a slightly descending blow at impact, to give the shot more backspin and control. (There may be occasions, however, when extreme wind conditions or difficult lies may call for the ball to be played farther forward or back than described here.)

LESSON: Common One-Plane Setup Faults and Their Corrections

For golfers trying to adopt the one-plane setup, I have noticed that the following errors are the most common:

1. The hands are positioned too far ahead of the ball at address (this is a key error that usually leads to all the others).
2. Shoulders are often too open in relation to the target line, while the hips are often too closed.
3. Too much weight is put on the left or forward foot.
4. Spine angle is too upright. At the same time, the player's shoulders (rather than the spine) tend to be slumped forward.
5. Spine angle is tilted to the left (when viewed from a face-on angle).
6. Hands are too high and are "reaching" for the ball.

Photo 2.6 One-plane setup fault: face-on view

Photo 2.7 One-plane setup fault: down-target-line view

In correcting these setup faults, as well as in correcting faulty motions in the swing itself, I want to introduce the concept of overcorrection. I have found that in getting a player to correct any fault, it is essential for the player to overcorrect that fault for a period of time in order to get the adjustment to take hold. I've found that invariably, the player who starts out by simply trying to make the correction accurately will, over time, always have a tendency to revert back to his or her old faulty setup or swing movement. That's why I encourage players to practice overcorrecting the various positions or movements slightly.

I also think it is imperative that you practice your overcorrections in front of a mirror to make sure that you are slightly exaggerating them. You'll find that out on the course, you'll always have a tendency to go back to what has been comfortable in the past. So keep overcorrecting and checking in the mirror to make sure you are doing so. Gradually, the adjustment will take hold out on the golf course.

That said, you must correct your setup flaws by doing the following:

Photo 2.8 One-plane correct setup: face-on view

1. First and foremost, move your hands farther back toward the center of your body (opposite the left seam of your trouser zipper). Also, you should have the top of the grip pointing midway between your forearms, rather than having the grip pointing more or less along the plane of your left forearm as the majority of right-handed golfers do.

2. When you move the hands back in relation to your body, it automatically helps you move your shoulders into a squarer position. Based on my teaching experience, I find that golfers who address the ball with the

hands well in front unwittingly open their shoulders to the target line at the same time. To prove how true this is, start with your hands in an exaggerated forward position, then move them back to nearly opposite your body's center. Immediately, you'll discover that your left shoulder moves out more toward the ball, so that an imaginary line drawn across both your shoulders is squarer to the target line.

3. Placing too much weight on your left or forward foot also tends to correlate with having your hands too far ahead. The one-plane golfer should feel that the body's weight is almost evenly distributed between the feet. The only reason I suggest that you have slightly more weight on your forward foot is that the one-plane swing creates, by definition, a much wider swing arc than a two-plane swing. Because the arc is naturally wider, you don't want to have most of the weight on your right (rear) foot. This would encourage an arc that becomes so wide that you "fall off" the ball on the backswing.

Photo 2.9 One-plane correct setup: down-target-line view

4. Make sure you bend forward from the hips at an angle of 30 to 45 degrees (depending on your height and the length of the club). Here's a tip that will help you to bend from the hips, as opposed to slumping forward from the waist: Stand in an upright position, then draw your shoulder blades downward and inward. Now bend forward. You'll see that with your shoulder blades pulled down, you are forced to bend your entire torso forward, as opposed to merely slumping the shoulders forward.

Remember to check that a line drawn perpendicular to your spine falls into the center of the 48-inch zone outside the ball. This point in particular is one where you might need to emphasize an overcorrection to ultimately get it just right.

5. If your hands are too far ahead at address, you will also tend to tilt your spine angle to the left, or toward the target. Again, if you move your hands back as described, that leftward spine lean will be eliminated as well. But again, check it in the mirror.

6. Looking at your posture in the mirror from a side view, relax your arms and hands so that they drop down and in, somewhat closer to your body. From this angle, your hands should be directly under your chin.

Fact Versus Feel

The setup adjustments I have described may not sound that difficult to make. However, any changes you make in the setup and swing, even if they are in reality fairly slight, will feel as if they are enormous. I'd like to stress that at first, any setup or swing adjustments should feel huge. If they don't, it means you aren't making a sufficient correction.

One **fact** that will result from the setup directions described will be that you are looking down at the ball from a very different angle. Instead of looking somewhat back to the ball with your head in front of it, you will be looking at the ball from slightly behind it. While this is fine, it will take some getting used to. Keep overcorrecting so that your spine is straight and, particularly on tee shots, you are looking more from behind the ball.

Likewise, when you move your hands to a position slightly behind the ball for a teed-up driver, the change in the **feel** of the setup will be enormous. You might have the sensation that when you swing you will inevitably hit way behind the ball. Trust me, when you apply the correct one-plane swing mechanics, you won't. Likewise, it may **feel** as though you are bent forward way too much from the hips. Peter Jacobsen has said it almost feels like he is bending forward at a

90-degree angle and laying his torso and head on a table. Of course that's not true but, like Peter, you will need to **feel** an overcorrection for a time until the new spine angle at address becomes second nature.

Once you have incorporated the correct elements of the one-plane setup and posture into your game, you will find it much easier to develop the one-plane backswing, the subject of the next chapter.

The One-Plane Backswing

In this chapter, I describe the ideal movements of the one-plane backswing, breaking down the first half of the total action into body movements and positions followed by arm and club movements and positions. In addition, I discuss the "packages" of flaws that amateurs (and to some degree, even the pros) most commonly make during the first segment of the swing. Usually when a golfer gets off track in one specific area, the flaw sets off a chain reaction in which other errors also crop up. (This is what we saw in the previous chapter, where the golfer whose hands are too far ahead of the club at address also tends to have other setup flaws because of this particular one.) After explaining a common fault, I describe the type of ball flight that most commonly occurs as a result. Furthermore, in the Fact Versus Feel segment at the end of each lesson, I review the realities and sensations you will experience as you implement these new swing moves into your one-plane backswing. Finally, I complete my instructional message by listing drills that will help you to understand and accomplish the swing moves.

Part One: Model One-Plane Backswing Body Movements

Starting from the ideal setup and posture, the one-plane golfer should focus on turning the shoulders as fully as possible. A line across the top of your shoulders should remain at right angles to your spine throughout the turn (both on the

Photo 3.1 One-plane shoulder turn in the zone

backswing and the downswing). This means you are making a true turn of the shoulders, with no tilting; when you have completed the shoulder turn to the top of the backswing, a line drawn across your shoulders should be well within the zone we have talked about, which extends from the ball to a point 48 inches beyond it. (In a perfect shoulder turn, the shoulders should now point to the same spot within the zone that a line drawn perpendicular to your spine at address pointed to.)

However, it is okay if at the top of the backswing the shoulders point, as a result of a spine lowering during the backswing, to a position in the zone nearer the ball. Just never let the shoulder angle drift outward toward the outside of the zone.

You should not consciously restrict the turn of the hips on the backswing. However, your hip turn will automatically be restricted by the setup posture I have outlined. As you recall, your shoulders started from a more bent-forward or downward-tilted position than your hips were in at address. Therefore, as you execute the backswing, your shoulders will be turning on a fairly upright plane; meanwhile, your hips are turning on a more horizontal plane, closer to the movement of a merry-go-round. This difference between the planes of the shoulder and the hip turns acts as a restrictor or governor to the hip turn. So let the hips turn. As long as you are actively turning your shoulders as far around as you can, the hips will gradually begin to turn also; because of the bent-over spine restriction, they will turn only about half as much as your shoulders, and that's fine.

As you turn your body to the top in the one-plane backswing, your weight distribution should actually stay the same as it was at address, which is to say, evenly distributed between the feet or even slightly favor-

Photo 3.2 One-plane centered weight distribution

ing the left or front foot. This advice surprises a lot of students, who are under the assumption that you must actively shift much of your weight onto the right (rear) foot as you swing back. Not so! As your upper body turns, your spine should remain steady and there must be no sway to the right or to the left.

As I pointed out in *The Plane Truth for Golfers*, the one-plane golfer will have a wide swing arc because the path of the arms and the club will follow a relatively flatter plane, more around the body. If you added an extreme weight shift and a sway away from the target to your backswing, your arc would become much too wide and out of control. So as you approach the top you should feel as though your weight is staying toward the insides of both feet, rather than shifting onto the rear foot.

Ideally, your spine angle should remain the same, when viewed from down-target, as it was at address. As mentioned above, if you are to err at all, I would rather see you increase your spine angle (which is to say, lower your spine angle even more) as you reach the top of the backswing. Never stand up and lose spine angle. Also, when viewed from a face-on angle, your spine tilt should remain perfectly vertical. If any error, it is acceptable for the spine to actually tilt a tiny bit left, or toward the target. But as with any major shifting of weight to the right, I consider it "Death Valley" for a one-plane golfer's spine to tilt to the right during the backswing, as this also will make the swing too flat and the arc overly wide.

LESSON: Correcting a Reverse Pivot Problem

The reverse pivot is one of the most common swing problems among all golfers. First, this player tends to tilt the shoulders during the backswing, with the left shoulder working down too much and the right shoulder tilting up.

But this player does not actually turn the shoulders sufficiently around the spine. In accompaniment with this fault, the player allows his or her hips to

slide laterally, away from the target, rather than remaining in place and simply responding to the full turn of the shoulders. Next, instead of swaying to the right along with the hips (which would not be desirable either), the upper torso actually leans noticeably more to the left than it was at address. This puts the majority of the weight on the left foot at the top of the backswing, in the classic reverse pivot position. From here, the player is most likely to swing down on a steep, out-to-in path. The results will include pulls, big slices, weak pop-ups that result from the clubhead digging in too deeply at or behind the ball, and steep topped shots (which mean the

Photo 3.3 One-plane reverse pivot fault

Photo 3.4 One-plane flatter shoulder turn into the outside part of the zone

ball is topped with the clubhead contacting the top of the ball while still on the way down). Very deep divots are also the result of a reverse pivot.

Here is what you must do to overcome a reverse pivot: First and foremost, you must turn your trunk and shoulders away from the ball as fully as you can. An excellent key is to try to turn until your back is squarely facing the target. When you complete this turn, a line across your shoulders should point to the outer 24 inches of the zone. (Most golfers will find it easier to make a fuller shoulder turn at this angle than if the shoulders pointed closer to the ball.)

Turning until your back faces the target is quite a large turn, I realize. However, if you turn the trunk as far around as you can (while keeping your weight centered as discussed), you will have alleviated your reverse pivot.

As you turn your shoulders away from the target, a second, simultaneous move is what I call "wallet pocket left." (I have listed a drill under this name in Chapter 5 for practice of this move.) This means you make a very slight bumping move to the left, or toward the target, with your left hip. This will alleviate the tendency to slide the hips away from the target. A good way to check this move is to have a friend stand behind you at address, holding the grip end of a club against the outside of your left hip. As you make your full upper-body turn, make sure that you keep your left hip in contact with the handle of the club.

Third, you must try to keep your weight evenly distributed as you reach the top of the backswing. If anything, in overcoming the reverse pivot, I'd like you to reach the top with a bit more weight on your right or rear foot. If you make a full, true turn and employ the wallet pocket left move explained above, chances are very good that you will have the desired weight distribution at the top; but you must be aware of it and "feel for it" if you have been a longtime reverse-pivot golfer. Finally, your spine tilt should point straight up and down when observed from a face-on view (instead of leaning toward the target). It's even okay for you to observe a slight tilt to the right, away from the target. This too should take care of itself if you have integrated the preceding points, but it's still a good idea to check on the spine angle either in a mirror or with a friend.

There are three drills that I recommend to help you overcome a reverse pivot. Rather than describe every drill in detail as we go along, because there are many of them, I will describe each of these drills for the one-plane swing in Chapter 5, and drills for the two-plane golfer in Chapter 9. Within these two chapters there will be subheadings that indicate the specific problem that each drill helps to correct. The first drill for the reverse pivot fault is the Wallet Pocket Left Drill already mentioned; the others are called the Club Across Shoulders Drill (Variation 1) and the Object-in-the-Sky Drill.

Fact Versus Feel

When you make these corrections for the reverse pivot, the **fact** is that you will have a dramatically different view of the ball at the top of the backswing, looking at it from more behind the ball with your right eye. (Make sure to check your corrected head and spine positions in a mirror.) You will also **feel** a number of body sensations. Your shoulder turn will **feel** very flat, or nearly horizontal; your left hip will **feel** as though it is much higher and much more to the left, toward the target; and you will **feel** as though your spine has tilted dramatically to the right. If you have these unusual "feels," great. When you put these moves into your backswing out on the course, your reverse pivot and the resulting mishits will disappear.

LESSON: Fixing an Overly Shallow Turn Fault

The opposite problem to a reverse pivot occurs when the one-plane golfer makes a turn of the trunk and shoulders that is too shallow—that is, a turn that is nearly horizontal, so that at the top of the backswing, a line across the shoulders points well beyond or outside the zone. (Such a shallow shoulder turn would be acceptable for the two-plane swinger, as we will discuss in detail in Chapter 6.)

The player whose shoulders turn in this manner can usually make a substantial turn. His or her tendency will be to reach the top with a high percentage of weight on the right or rear foot; the spine is tilted to the right (away from the

Photo 3.5 One-plane shallow turn fault

target) and the head has also moved in that direction; the spine angle (when viewed from down-target) is likely to have risen rather than remained constant; and often, the player's right elbow will be unusually low, just above the belt line. The player with this problem does not display the hip slide to the right as in the reverse pivot.

The player exhibiting these faults will end up with ball flights that are basically opposite to those of the reverse pivot player. This is to say that the clubhead will be delivered to the ball on a very shallow arc, and one that approaches the ball from well inside the target line. (Teachers are constantly referring to students who swing from the outside-in and slice the ball. But it is also true that swinging the clubhead from too far inside the target line creates just as many, albeit opposite, types of mishits.) The results of this shallow, inside-out arc will include thin shots, catching the turf behind the ball (often referred to as a "drop-kick"), pushed shots, hooks, and shallow tops (meaning the leading edge of the clubface contacts the upper half of the ball after it has started moving up). This golfer will take little or no divot on any shots.

To correct the problem of the shallow turn, you must learn to turn the shoulders on a steeper plane than you are accustomed to. While turning your shoulders fully, do so on an angle so that, if you put a club shaft across your shoulders at the top of the backswing, the club shaft would point to the inside 24 inches of the zone. (See Club Across Shoulders Drill (Variation 2) in the one-plane drills in Chapter 5.) A note of warning: Make sure that your spine is tilted forward sufficiently at address so that you can turn into the inside of the zone while keeping your shoulders at right angles to your spine. Often, the horizontal shoulder-turn stems from having the spine too upright to begin with.

When the shoulder turn is steeper, the overall swing motion will become a bit narrower, which is what you want in this case. When you make this more desirable shoulder turn, you'll note that your right elbow is automatically raised, the point of the elbow moving somewhat up the seam line on the side of your shirt. One of the causes of this problem is holding the right elbow too low and pointed down, which does not allow the right shoulder to turn up and behind you on plane within the zone. So make sure you are not holding the right elbow down. (Note photo in Club Across Shoulders Drill (Variation 2) in Chapter 5.) The hips as noted should be maintaining a stable position, and you will need to consciously check to make sure that at least 50 percent of your weight stays on your left or forward foot. If you do this, your spine angle when viewed from in front should remain straight or angle a bit to your left (toward the target). The one-planer should never allow the spine to tilt to the right during the swing. Likewise, have a friend observe your spine angle from a down-target vantage point. You must hold this spine angle constant. If anything, I'd rather see you lower your spine angle a tiny bit rather than raise it.

Fact Versus Feel

If you've been turning your upper body too horizontally, it's a **fact** that at the top of your backswing, you will be viewing the ball from a noticeably different angle. Your head will now be even with the ball, so that you are looking down on it with your left eye from slightly in front of it. Check in the mirror to make sure this head position is accurate.

At first, the correction will make you **feel** as though your shoulder turn is much too steep and your swing is very upright and narrow. Again, you must fight through this **feel** in order to get to where the correction will take hold. Tom Pernice Jr., one of the PGA Tour players I work with, has a unique way of ingraining this steeper feel. Tom, who has a natural tendency to make a shallow turn and swing the club too flat, waggles the club in a very upright manner—lifting the club, his right shoulder, and his right elbow—to remind himself to turn his shoulders on a fairly steep plane on the backswing. You should also **feel** as if your spine is tilted well toward the target and that your weight most definitely favors your forward foot, even though your actual amount of spine tilt and weight distribution toward the left in reality are only slight.

Part Two: Model One-Plane Backswing Arms and Club Movements and Positions

Let's continue on to the movements of the arms and the clubhead during the one-plane golf swing. In the ideal one-plane swing, the arms will swing around the body as the body turns on both the backswing and the downswing. As you turn in the backswing, your right elbow will move upward and backward in a piston-like motion. This up-and-back movement of the right elbow allows the left arm to cross over and swing tight against the front of the chest, where it should remain through the completed backswing.

Let's look at a checkpoint early in the backswing, when the club shaft moves to a point where it is parallel to the ground, at about hip height. (A long iron is best to illustrate the point I'm going to make.) At this stage, the club shaft should be parallel to your target line. When viewed from down-target, the club shaft should be directly over the insteps of your shoes (as opposed to being well outside your toes). Also, the leading edge of the clubface should be square to the plane of your swing. Please note that I said "square to the plane of your swing," *not* that the leading edge of the club should be pointing straight up, as most students (and many teachers) believe it should be.

There is a big difference between the leading edge pointing straight up and having it point square to the plane of your swing. Let me explain.

Imagine that the plane of your swing (and your clubhead) will trace the path of a hula hoop that is resting at about a 50-degree angle, roughly halfway between being completely upright and lying flat on the ground. Imagine the clubhead starting on the ground and facing the target. Now imagine the club moving back to the point in the backswing I've described above, so that the shaft is parallel to the target line and about hip high. If there has been no manipulation whatsoever of the clubhead up to now, where would the leading edge of the clubface be pointing? To

Photo 3.6 One-plane midpoint backswing with shaft over insteps and clubface square to the plane

the observer looking from a down-target view, the leading edge would not point straight up. Instead it would be pointing both up and toward the target line, or to put it another way, to about 45 degrees. It is in this position that the clubface itself is square to the plane of the swing. And from here, you can clearly see that the golfer would have to use forearm or hand rotation to turn the clubhead so that its toe points straight up, and you would see that this manipulation represents an opening of the clubface. So, at this checkpoint the leading edge of the club should be at the 45 degrees, halfway between toe-up and facedown, so it remains square to the plane of the swing.

Photo 3.7 One-plane clubface square to the plane

If you are having any difficulty in visualizing what I have described, a good drill that will help you understand it, as well as get the feeling for the movement of the arms in the early part of the backswing, is the Bucket Drill (see Chapter 5).

A Key Digression

I would like to tell you something that I think you'll find fascinating, but more important, something that will help you to understand the golf swing in a way you never have before.

I have just shown you what a square clubface is when the shaft is parallel to the target line. What, then, is a truly square clubface at the top of the backswing? Well, imagine the clubhead continuing up that imaginary hula hoop that represents the plane of the swing. If you could observe yourself from down-target, you would see that the clubface would be pointing straight at you, which is also to say, directly away from the target and what we in golf would declare as being 90 degrees closed.

Photo 3.8 One-plane top of backswing "square" is actually 90 degrees open to plane.

Now I ask you, does anyone who plays the game, be it pro or hacker, have the clubhead in this clubface-pointing-behind-you position at the top of the backswing? Definitely not. Where do most golfers have it? Well, we usually say the clubface should be pointing about halfway between straight to the sky and pointing in the same direction that you, the player, are facing (the target line). Teachers (and students) have come to define this as a square clubface position at the top.

Well, you have just seen in the previous paragraph where a clubface that is truly square to the swing plane would be pointing. What, then, is the truth about the clubface position that most teachers are trying to get their students in at the top? This clubface position is *90 degrees open in relation to the plane of the swing.*

I realize this may be difficult for you to grasp. I can assure you that I have done hundreds of teaching seminars attended by many fine and conscientious teachers, and every time I explain this I see stares ranging from completely blank to utter disbelief. But it is true. What happens is that from the midpoint of the backswing to the top, we rotate the club with the forearms into a position

Photo 3.9 One-plane right hand square to plane at backswing midpoint

Photo 3.10 One-plane right hand rotated 90 degrees open to the plane at top of backswing

that, depending on the grip, is approximately 90 degrees open in relation to the plane of the swing. Why do we strive to do this, and perhaps more important, how do we do it?

Well, the reason we rotate the clubface to this wide-open position is, quite simply, in order to cock the wrists and to complete the backswing. If you tried to keep the clubface square to the path of the backswing, you wouldn't have a complete backswing. Or I should say, your backswing would have to come to a halt when your hands had gotten just beyond waist height. Given the human anatomy, you could not cock your wrists and continue to move the clubhead square to your swing plane. Granted, you could stop your swing right there and leave it at that. I guarantee that you would hit the ball straight, but from this position you might not be able to hit the ball 100 yards.

So, what do we do? We continue turning the body and allowing the club to swing back. How do we get the club to swing all the way back? By rotating the forearms in a clockwise fashion and cocking the wrists, which allows the arms and club to continue back (and at the same time opens the clubface in relation to the swing plane). You will note that in making this clockwise rotation, your left arm remains pinned to your chest while your right elbow lifts slightly up and away from your side. When your club reaches the top, the clubface should be in either a square position (mind you, using the standard definition of square), or slightly closed (again by that standard definition).

If you are supple enough to reach a point at the top of the backswing where the club shaft reaches parallel to the ground, the club shaft should point either parallel to the target line or slightly laid off, in other words, pointing left of the target. (If your swing does not reach parallel on the backswing, the club shaft will appear to point somewhat to the left of the target, and may appear to be more laid off, as I explained in *The Plane Truth for Golfers*. That said, a slightly laid-off position at the top is fine for the one-plane player.)

The preceding discussion is, I believe, key for you to understand, particularly if you wish to develop a high-quality one-plane swing. And because most golfers, up until now at least, have misunderstood what squareness of the clubface means throughout the swing, they usually must overcome a variety of errors in executing the backswing. Let's look at some of them.

LESSON: Correcting an Arms in Front of Body Position

The key backswing error for the one-planer is to allow the arms to stay in front of the body, rather than pulling the right elbow upward and backward so that the left arm crosses over the front of the chest. Instead, the right elbow stays in front of the right side and points straight down at the top. This non-pulling action of the right elbow forces the left arm to roll upward and away from the player's chest. Halfway back, this player will either have the club shaft too far inside and not parallel to the target line or will have the club shaft parallel to the target line as we would like, but too much away from him or her, over a point well outside the toes rather than over the insteps.

Also, most players will have rolled the clubface with the hands into what we now see is an open position, with the leading edge pointing straight up or even over rather than angled to the right when viewed from behind.

Photo 3.11 One-plane arms in front fault with club shaft too far inside

Photo 3.12 One-plane arms in front fault with club shaft too far away and clubface too open

One-plane players with these backswing flaws are setting themselves up to either have the club stuck behind them, coming from too much inside with the clubface too open, or having the club swinging on a correct path with the club-face too open. The problem with both these mistakes (club stuck behind and correct path with clubface too open) is that they require excessive hand action during impact to just hit the ball. This need for excessive hand action results in great clubface squaring inconsistencies. The resulting ball flights are shots right and left: slices and hooks.

Here's how to overcome the problem of keeping the arms in front of the chest: You need to swing your left arm across your chest on the backswing. In order to do that, however, you must move your right or rear elbow up and back in the proper manner. When you are set up over the ball and ready to swing, move your right elbow vigorously upward and to the rear. Your right elbow should move up and back at about a 45-degree angle; when you've pulled

Photo 3.13 One-plane showing A position at address

Photo 3.14 One-plane closing the A

that elbow back as far as you can, your elbow joint should go back at least to the seam on the right side of your golf shirt, or slightly beyond that seam, if possible.

Some golfers have trouble visualizing this very important move. Let me explain it another way. If you were to stand in a down-target position behind a player at address, you could imagine that the upper part of the player's right arm, and the seam running up and down the right side of his shirt, form the two outside lines of the letter A.

When the player moves the right elbow back and up as I have described, he will be moving the upper arm in such a way that he closes the gap between the two prongs of the letter A. So a good way to visualize this move is to think of closing the A with the movement of your right elbow.

To help you develop the feel of this right-elbow-back movement, see the Arms Around Body Drill, the Bucket Drill, the X Drill, Right Arm Pointer Drill (Variation 1), and the Close the A Drill in Chapter 5. (Each of these drills has variations that apply to both the backswing and the downswing of the one-plane swing; you need only concern yourself with the parts pertaining to the backswing arm movements at this point.)

When you make this aggressive, right-elbow-back move, what happens? Well, if both hands are holding onto the club, your left arm will be pulled up and across the front of your chest. That's how your arms must act in a one-plane golf swing. As you continue to turn your body in the backswing, make sure your left arm stays tight to your chest, hugging the lower part of your pectoral muscles. A very good drill to help you keep that left arm pinned to your chest is the Glove Under Arm Drill (see Chapter 5).

In the first half of the backswing, you should avoid any rotation of the left arm. But in the second half, you must rotate both your left forearm and your right forearm in order to allow your arms to keep up with the turn of the torso, and thus keep the club moving all the way to the top. When I say the right wrist rotates, the right forearm rotates along with it. If it helps you to think of the entire right forearm rotating, rather than just the right wrist, that imagery is fine too. An excellent way to dissect this movement of the arms and the club in the second half of the backswing is to practice the backswing portions of the X Drill (Variation 1) and the Club Set Drill, also in Chapter 5.

Fact Versus Feel

As you're working into the second half of the backswing, it is a **fact** that your right elbow must work slightly up and away from the right side of your chest. This is necessary to complete the backswing. I would rather see you allow the right elbow to get too far up and away to **feel** a "flying right elbow" than to limit the backswing by holding the elbow down and not moving it up and back enough.

LESSON: Remedy for Swinging the Club Inside Too Quickly

Another problem of the would-be one-planer is getting the club moving too quickly to the inside, a movement that is then followed by a lift of the arms to get the club up to the top. This inside-then-up move is quite common.

Usually the player is moving his or her arms correctly; however, the hips are turning too early, too fast, and too much, resulting in the club moving back in a flat, merry-go-round fashion rather than halfway between Ferris wheel and merry-go-round. Once this player gets to that crucial halfway-back point in the backswing, there is only one thing he or she can do, and that is to lift the club up with the arms to the top. When this player does reach a full top-of-backswing position, most often the club shaft will be pointing across the line, or to the right of the target.

Usually, this player's downswing path mirrors the backswing so that he or she comes into the ball on a very shallow, inside-to-out angle. Fat shots (if the club catches the ground early), thin shots (where the leading edge never reaches the ground), shallow topped shots (topped on the upswing), shots pushed to the right, and big hooks to the left can result. This player takes very little if any divot.

Photo 3.15 One-plane with the club too much inside at midpoint of backswing

Photo 3.16 One-plane with club shaft across the line

Photo 3.17 One-plane slight drag at start of backswing

Photo 3.18 One-plane start of backswing with delayed hip turn

I would advise the player who goes too far inside too early to first create a slight dragging action during the take-away.

By this I mean the hands will start back just an instant before the clubhead moves back from the ball. This tiny drag will set the club shaft so that it is just about in line with the right forearm, instead of pointing to a line in between the arms. This slight drag motion is excellent insurance, if you will, against whipping the clubhead immediately to the inside.

The second, and I believe most critical point for this player, is to make sure the hip turn is restricted until the second half of the backswing. The sequence of movements must be arms and then the shoulders, with no hip turn until late in the backswing.

Last, once you have reached the midpoint of the backswing, you should rotate the right wrist and the left forearm in order to set the club more to the left at the top of the backswing. When you rotate the left forearm and right wrist, make certain that the right elbow does not jump out in front of you. Instead it should move slightly up and away from your right side. Also, make sure to extend your left arm along the plane of the lower-right club shaft line, as discussed in the X Drill (Variation 1) in Chapter 5.

Two other drills that will help the one-plane golfer with this backswing problem are the Club Set Drill and the Right Arm Pointer Drill (Variation 1).

Fact Versus Feel

The key **fact** in the backswing movement is that you must continue to move the right elbow upward and behind you, with the elbow joint reaching or even getting slightly behind the seam on the side of your shirt. When you do this, the left arm must cross over the front of your chest much earlier and much more fully than you are accustomed to. This will very likely produce some very different sensations for you. Early in the backswing, it will seem as if the club is very far in front of the hands; another way of putting this is that it will **feel** as if the clubhead is lagging rather than being whipped quickly inside the target line, as it may have previously been doing. During the first half of the backswing, the clubface will **feel** very closed. As a total movement, your arm swing on the backswing will definitely **feel** much shorter than usual. You might get the sensation that you haven't done enough to get the club back as far as you need to. Don't worry. As long as you're turning your upper body concurrently with performing the correct one-plane movement of the arms, you're doing plenty. What you are not doing anymore, and thus not feeling, is lifting the club during the second half of your backswing, a move that actually does nothing except make it more difficult for you to find the correct plane on the downswing.

As you reach the top of the one-plane backswing, and particularly if your club shaft was crossing the line as we talked about earlier, you will **feel** as if you have made an extremely flat backswing, and the club shaft will feel very low behind you. PGA Tour veteran Bob Tway says that when he swings back correctly, the backswing feels extremely short and it seems as though his left arm is somewhere down near his waist. Rest assured that it is not. It is true that at the top of the backswing, the club shaft will be slightly lower than it used to be, probably crossing behind the top of your head (if you were observing yourself from face-on) rather than being a bit above your head. This is the result of making an on-plane, one-plane backswing in which you've swung the club along the plane set by your shoulders at address, with no lifting of the club—the flatter plane we have theorized about earlier. The resulting position of the club is probably just two to three inches lower than it was in the past. However, it will seem to be different by light-years, and if you are now executing the one-plane backswing perfectly, it should **feel** like a difference in light-years. Don't be thrown off by this. You might reach the top, panic, and say to yourself, "What's going to happen when I come down? The club doesn't feel like it's in the same place. Will I even hit the ball?" Stop worrying. Instead, congratulate yourself. By making a correct one-plane backswing, you have put yourself in position to hit golf shots like you never have before. Once you have learned the correct backswing, learning the downswing will not be very difficult because, as you will see, it is essentially a mirror image of what you have done on the backswing. I promise you, once you learn to put the entire one-plane swing together, you will be able to hit consistently solid, straight, and on-target golf shots by the hour.

So let's forge ahead to the next chapter, where you will learn to execute a textbook one-plane downswing.

The One-Plane Downswing

In the ideal one-plane top-of-backswing position, your shoulders will be turned 90 degrees from your address position (or to your personal maximum if you are unable to reach a 90-degree shoulder turn). Your hips will also have turned, but only in response to the shoulder turn, which means they will have turned about half as much as the shoulders. Your cocked right elbow has pulled the club back and your left (forward) arm is pinned across your chest. Meanwhile, the clockwise rotation of your left arm and right wrist has brought the club up to the top on a single continuous plane line. Your club shaft should be pointing either directly at the target or slightly to the left of it (slightly laid off).

You are now perfectly poised to swing down and through and hit a great golf shot, provided you strive for the following ideal downswing positions.

Part One: Model One-Plane Downswing Body Movements

Many teachers tell their students to think of the golf swing as a simple one-two movement, with "one" representing the backswing turn and "two" representing the downswing and follow-through. While I understand the value of keeping instruction as simple as possible, I'd like to insert one small but important point. Yes, to develop a sense of rhythm in your swing, you should think of the backswing turn in terms of your part one. However, I would like you to insert what I call your two-move, just before you unfurl your downswing. This two-move is simply a small bumping move with your left side, which moves a bit more of your weight onto your left foot. This two-move is almost imperceptible; don't overdo it and slide your body laterally. Just try to stand a little more on the left leg as the "two" count in your swing. This small move then activates the downswing and follow-through (which is now your "three" count).

You should try to turn your shoulders and your entire torso a full 180 degrees from where they were at the top of the

Photo 4.1 One-plane "two" move

backswing, back down through impact and up to the finish. (Let me point out right now that when we discuss arm and club movements of the one-plane downswing, I will be interjecting some key additional points as regards the arm movement.) Concurrent with this, your weight should be moving smoothly forward onto your left or lead foot.

For now, there are just a couple of points I would like you to be aware of as regards the body through impact and completion of the one-plane swing. At and through impact, it's important to make sure that you maintain the forward bend of the spine as you had it at address. If anything, the one-plane swinger is better off if he or she lowers the spine angle slightly (as Hogan did) rather than raise it. Also, you want to keep your spine straight when viewed from a face-on angle, tilting neither toward nor away from the target.

Photo 4.2 One-plane near impact with correct forward bend of the spine angle

Photo 4.3 One-plane correct spine position with no side tilt

Your finish position should be a very natural one. Through and past impact, your weight should have naturally flowed onto your left foot until it is almost completely there at the end of the follow-through.

I hope you will be able to assimilate the moves of the one-plane downswing without slipping into any pitfalls. However, because all of the preceding instructions seem quite new and unusual, I've found that my students sometimes do have problems putting the one-plane downswing together. For this reason, I am going to provide three separate prob-

Photo 4.4 One-plane correct finish with weight fully onto left foot

lem scenarios regarding the body movement in the one-plane downswing and explain how to correct them.

LESSON: Curing the Problems of Raising the Spine Angle and Thrusting the Hips

In this case, the player's hips, rather than both the hips and the upper torso, dominate the downswing. Instead of employing an almost imperceptible two-move, the golfer shifts the left or forward hip laterally at least several inches toward the target and also moves it somewhat outward, toward the ball. As a result, the player's weight shifts rather violently onto the front or forward foot. At the same time, this player's spine angle usually rises up. This means that the shoulder turn is going to become too level, too much like a merry-go-round, so that a line across the shoulders at impact points well outside the zone. Also, and perhaps more important, the shoulders have not continued to rotate forcefully through and beyond impact. The results of this set of errors is usually a very shallow, inside-out clubhead path that produces both fat and thinned shots, shallow topped shots, straight pushes to the right, and big hooks. The player making these errors usually doesn't take much divot.

A lot of this player's problem can be traced to a movement of the arms that is too much up-and-down like a Ferris wheel, and too much inside-to-out rather than inside to along the target line and back to the inside. The lateral sliding of the hips along with the erect spine angle is a means for the body to support this upright and out-of-line Ferris wheel arm action. This player must remember to make the rotation of the chest and shoulders a more dominant movement of the downswing. It might help this player to think in terms of keeping the left shoulder moving slightly down and to the left at the start of the downswing. Peter Jacobsen, who as you probably know by now is great at creating visual images, refers to this as his "unicorn" move. Peter imagines he is a unicorn and that he is going to point the horn on his head down and to the left at the start of the downswing. This move, which will increase the spine angle rather than decrease it, is an exaggeration, of course. However, it will help the player to keep the hips stable, making only that slight bump of the hip we refer to as the "two-move." There should be no further lateral hip movement, and the rotation of the hips should merely follow that of the upper torso.

Photos 4.5–4.6 One-plane fault of a raised spine angle and thrusting hips

There are several drills that will help you to assimilate the correct one-plane downswing. These include the Arms Around Body Drill (Variation 2), which is particularly helpful if the player is slicing or shanking because the right elbow is leading the downswing; the Club Across Shoulders Drill (Variation 3); the Brute Drill, which helps you get the feel of shifting weight properly onto your left foot; and the Object-in-the-Sky Drill. All of these are described in detail in Chapter 5.

Fact Versus Feel

Fact: If you successfully correct the tendency to allow your spine angle to rise up during the swing, you will have a dramatically different view of the ball as you begin your follow-through. You'll be looking at it from a lower angle and with your eyes closer to the target line than they previously were.

Photo 4.7 One-plane club shaft swinging back to the inside just after impact

There are quite a few different "feels" that occur with your corrected spine angle on the downswing and follow-through. For example, at the start of the downswing you will probably **feel** as though your left shoulder is too low (because previously, it had gotten so high). In fact, your entire spine bend will feel dramatically steeper. It is steeper, but once again, the feel is always more dramatically different than the actual adjustment in the position really looks.

Nearly all of my students **feel** as if they are coming over the top at the start of this downswing. You're not.

As you swing down and through, you will **feel** like your arms are down around your waist and that they are moving around your body like a merry-go-round instead of your old Ferris wheel motion. They will **feel** too far to your left, too far around you, much too fast. Trust me when I tell you they are not! A great example of this is Olin Browne on the PGA Tour. People who see how quickly his clubhead comes back inside the target line after impact always say, "Wow, he must have pulled that shot a mile left!" Yet all that Browne is doing is continuing to swing along a consistent, hula hoop–type, in-to-in swing plane.

And as his success on the PGA Tour has proven, he is a very accurate ball striker. When you feel like your arms are moving quickly to the inside past impact, it probably means that for the first time in your life, your swing is staying on-plane beyond impact.

Concurrent with this, you will also probably **feel** like your left hip has rotated too much behind you past impact. People often refer to this as "spinning out." Again, as long as your lower body is rotating in response to the turn of your upper torso, it should feel like your hip has rotated much more to the left. Finally it should **feel** as though your upper torso (not your hips) is the main motor or force driving the downswing.

LESSON: Curing Loss of Spine Angle, Hip Turn Backing Up, and Outside-In Downswing Plane Problems

This player also tends to raise his or her spine angle during the downswing, but for essentially the opposite reason as in the previous example. As the downswing begins, the hips actually back up—that is, shift laterally away from the target. When this happens, the spine angle automatically lifts up, and the spine usually tilts toward the target, with the head also moving in the direction of the target.

Photo 4.8 One-plane fault of spine lift, too flat a shoulder turn, hips "backing up," and outside-in swing path

Photo 4.9 One-plane with backing-up hip turn and spine tilting to the left

As the downswing continues, this player usually will turn the upper torso sufficiently. However, with the loss of spine angle, the shoulders are turning on too flat a plane, a line across them pointing beyond the zone.

As a result of these problems (the primary one being the backing up of the hips and a reverse weight shift), this player is the classic slice-hitter. His or her swing must come into the ball on an outside-in plane and at a very steep angle. The results are varied and seldom good: Fat, popped-up shots with the club digging into the turf behind the ball, steep tops with the ball hit on the downswing, huge left-to-right slices, and occasionally (when the clubface gets flipped through impact so that it's square to the swing path) big pulls to the left. This player consistently gouges out deep divots rather than a nice shallow nip from the turf.

Most of this player's problem can be traced to a faulty motion of the arms in which he or she swings outward and downward. Meanwhile, the lower body gets

Photo 4.10 One-plane correct "two" move

Photo 4.11 One-plane increased spine angle and steeper shoulder turn

Photo 4.12 One-plane slight spine tilt to the right at impact

out of position (the hips backing up) in order to support the upright, out-to-in swing motion.

To solve the problem, you must make your arms move more like a merry-go-round. That is, they must move in a more rounded, inside-to-inside plane. In order to accomplish this, I would first remind you to start the downswing with the slight "stand on the left foot" bump move.

While doing this, do not allow your head to move much toward the target. Then, throughout the downswing, you must continue to move your weight toward the left or forward foot. While this is happening, you should try to turn your shoulders more vertically, around the fixed angle of the spine. (If anything, you may need to increase the angle of the spine on the downswing.)

Also, when swinging down, your spine tilt, if anything, should be angled slightly to the right or away from the target when viewed from face-on. This helps to ensure that your hips will not back up during the downswing.

If you are struggling with these faults, you will probably benefit most from repeated use of the following drills: the Club Across Shoulders Drill (Variation 2); the Brute Drill; and the Arms Around Body Drill (Variation 2). (See Chapter 5 for a description of each drill.)

Fact Versus Feel

You will, in **fact**, be looking at the ball from a much different angle as you follow through, with the eyes at a 45-degree angle to the flight of the ball, looking at it from more directly behind. Again, there are a number of feels that will seem radical until you get accustomed to them. The slight lateral movement of your left side toward the target during the "stand on your left foot" might **feel** larger and more forceful than it is, and your weight will **feel** tremendously on your left foot because you are used to backing your hips away from the target and putting your weight on your rear foot. Also, throughout and just past impact, your spine bend will and should **feel** dramatically steeper, bent more toward the ball. Your arms will **feel** as if they are moving low around your waist, from the inside to down the line at the target (Your arms will in **fact** be moving from inside to on-target to inside, but because you are so used to moving them outside-in, the

feel will be as if they are now swinging from inside to down the line). As you reach the finish, you should **feel** as though your left hip is higher than normal and that it is turned far more around you to your left.

As a final note on this problem, I should mention that sometimes the player who makes these corrections finds that he or she will start to hook or pull shots. If this happens to you, I recommend practicing the Object-in-the-Sky Drill in the reverse of the manner it is described in Chapter 5—that is, turning the torso vigorously on the follow-through side of the ball. Also, when working with the Arms Around Body Drill (Variation 2), work on releasing your right arm around to the left, but with the palm of that hand facing more upward than to the left.

Photo 4.13 One-plane near finish position with slight retained spine angle and hip tilt

LESSON: Alleviating Lateral Hip Slide and Shoulder Tilt Problems

The third problem that I typically see is the golfer who tilts the shoulders into the downswing, rather than turning them around the spine angle. For the right-handed golfer, this usually means dipping the right shoulder while the left shoulder works up. If you tilt your shoulders, it is not physically possible to turn your shoulders very far around your spine on either the backswing or the downswing.

In addition to this fault, the golfer will commonly slide the hips laterally toward the target, instead of allowing them to turn in response to the turn of the torso. Another way of putting it is that the player is making too big a two- move.

Also, although this player usually manages to maintain the spine's forward angle on the downswing, the player does tend to let his or her spine tilt to the right, or away from the target (usually in response to the lateral hip slide).

When these flaws occur, what will usually happen is that the player will get the club "stuck" behind the body. This is a term you may have heard Tiger

Photo 4.14 One-plane downswing shoulder tilt fault

Photo 4.15 One-plane shoulder tilt and excessive hip slide

Woods or other PGA Tour pros refer to from time to time. This means that at a point about halfway through the downswing, the club is too far behind the golfer and its clubface is much too open. The end result is a swing path that is very shallow and in-to-out through impact (in relation to the target line). Either fat or thin shots can occur, as well as out-and-out shallowly topped shots. Because of this inside-out path, the shot can either be pushed to the right (if the clubface matches up with the path of the swing) or can start right and hook badly left (if the clubface closes sharply in relation to the path by the instant of impact).

If you're trying to solve the hip slide/shoulder tilt problem, I'd advise you to do the following:

1. Make sure that the turn of your upper torso (chest and shoulders) dominates the downswing. You can rotate the torso as fast as you want, providing you keep your spine angled forward as you do so.
2. Avoid making the two-move with your hip, as I advise most players to do. Try to make the movement with your hips a completely circular movement, which should occur only in response to the uncoiling of your upper torso.

Photo 4.16 One-plane downswing with dominating shoulder turn and neutral spine tilt

3. Strive to keep your spine tilt neutral, not tilting right or left when viewed from directly in front.

I should add here that sometimes a player will work hard to make the correct one-plane downswing, and in fact will be doing everything very nearly correctly, only to find that his or her shots still either hook or slice. The Anti-Hook Grip Pressure Drill is a great remedy to eliminate that slight hook or fade: If you're drawing your shots, grip the club firmly with the base or heel of your right hand, at the lifeline, against the top of your left thumb as you swing through impact. If your shots are fading, then slightly reduce the pressure, with the lifeline of your right hand on the top of your left thumb.

Drills that will help the player fighting these faults are the Brute Drill and the Object-in-the-Sky Drill (on both the backswing and downswing directions, to make sure that your chest and not just your shoulders are turning); the Anti-Hook Grip Pressure Drill; and the Arms Around Body Drill (Variation 2). (All drills are described in Chapter 5.)

Fact Versus Feel

The **fact** of the matter is that if you turn your torso correctly away from and then down through the ball, your clubhead will be moving on a path that is inside the target line except for the instant when it is moving directly along the target line, which is at impact. This is true even though it may **feel** as though your shoulder turn on the downswing is bringing the club around from the outside-in. It will also **feel** as though you are swinging too flat, in other words, that your shoulder turn at impact is pointing beyond the zone. This is because you are used to the feeling of your shoulders tilting rather than turning as they should. In the same vein, you'll **feel** that your arms are swinging horizontally around your waist, like a merry-go-round, and that they are also swinging too much to the left. Your left hip will also **feel** as though it's turning too fast and too far to the left, or spinning out. It's not, but it feels that way because that sliding hip action is what you're accustomed to.

Likewise, you will **feel** as though the spine is tilting toward the target when it remains straight up and down and centered over the hips instead of tilted back to the right.

Part Two: Model One-Plane Downswing Arms and Club Movements and Positions

The ideal downswing movement of the arms will be a mirror image of everything you did on the backswing. On the backswing, you pulled your right elbow up and back so that it was opposite or beyond your right-side shirtsleeve, and then you cocked and rotated clockwise your right forearm upward so that your club could reach its top-of-the-backswing position. Now, as you start turning your hips and upper body in the downswing, you will simultaneously reposition the arms and club from the top by dropping and rotating your right forearm down from its cocked position. Simply drop your right forearm so your right hand moves toward your right pants pocket. Notice that as you make this move, your right wrist and your left forearm, while dropping, simultaneously rotate slightly in a counterclockwise fashion.

Photos 4.17–4.18 One-plane correct right forearm drop with right elbow still up and behind the right side

Some golfers prefer making this move with the right forearm dropping down while the right elbow stays up and behind (on or near the seam of the shirt). Tom Pernice Jr. uses a visual that he is placing the lid on a trash can with his right hand, while other golfers want to accomplish this by turning the left forearm counterclockwise so the left arm "rolls" down the chest and the right and left hands end up near the right hip on what I call the "inner circle."

At this point, something might be troubling you. "Did you say that I will reposition the arms and club from the top-of-backswing position simultaneous with the start of the downswing body turn?" you ask. "Wouldn't that mean that I am throwing or casting the club from the top? Isn't that what we're taught *not* to do? Aren't we supposed to hold back the wrists and the clubhead and delay the hit as much as possible?"

My responses, in order, to your very valid questions are as follows: yes, no, yes. Meaning yes, I do want you to reposition the arms and club immediately as you start the downswing, by rotating the left forearm and right forearm in a counterclockwise manner. And no, this does not mean you are casting or throwing the club from the top, as least as I would define casting or throwing. And yes, I understand that almost universally, golfers have been told to hold on to their arms and club until much later in the downswing in order to delay the hit as much as possible.

But I now want to explain to you why following this well-meaning advice is causing considerable damage to your effort to hit the ball solidly and straight all the time, knowing I am going be explaining something to you about the golf swing that is pretty technical. It is something I do not think you have ever heard or read before. It is information that has taken me almost my entire lifetime to fully grasp, and I believe it is the most important swing information you will ever receive. Now you know why you are attending Jim Hardy's Master Class.

The following vital information needs to be explained fully with the help of a story about the greatest technician of the golf swing in history: Ben Hogan.

Why Hogan Hooked

Every student of golf knows that Ben Hogan set the bar for golf shot-making excellence in the late 1940s through the mid-1950s. Hogan captured four U.S. Opens within a span of six years, two PGA Championships, two Masters wins, and the British Open in his only attempt there, in 1953 at Carnoustie Golf Club in Scotland. This magnificent record almost certainly would have been far greater if Hogan had not, at his career zenith in January 1949, been seriously injured in a near-fatal car-bus crash. The accident left him with a broken pelvis and damage to his legs that afterward often made walking 18 holes sheer misery. That Hogan possessed both the will and the skill to come back and win six more major championships is still, I believe, the most remarkable career achievement in golf history.

I might add that Hogan managed to accomplish what he did despite the fact that in his later competitive years, his putting gradually eroded to the point where he suffered a severe case of the yips. Being based in the Houston, Texas, area, I've had the opportunity to meet and talk in detail with many of Hogan's contemporaries, foremost among them Jackie Burke, himself the 1956 Masters champion. All of them have assured me that had Hogan been able to putt even decently from about 1954 on, he undoubtedly would have added several more major titles to his career record.

That said, many golf fans don't really know about all the lean years during which Hogan struggled mightily to survive as a professional golfer. Hogan, along with Sam Snead and Byron Nelson, began competing professionally in the 1930s. Of the three, Hogan was the least successful for a number of years. Of course, back then, the PGA golf tour was nothing like it is today. Usually only a handful of top finishers even earned a paycheck for their week's work. On several occasions, Hogan had to drop off the tour to work as a card dealer in high-stakes games back in Texas in order to cobble together enough money to try the tournament circuit again.

Hogan struggled valiantly with his game and finally broke through to win his first professional tournament in 1941. Through the 1940s his career gained momentum, but Hogan's tee-to-green game was still erratic. A man of small stature, Hogan back then was able to hit the ball a long way because he had a very long swing (much longer than in his prime years) and because he had very fast hands through the hitting zone. By this I mean that Hogan rotated the clubface from a very open position as he entered the hitting zone to a closed position shortly after impact. Hogan generated great clubhead speed, and when his timing was on he was capable of winning tournaments. When his timing

Photo 4.19 Hogan's early career one-plane fault of right elbow too low and in front of right hip with the club shaft off-plane

was just a little off, however, Hogan was subject to hitting uncontrollable hooks, and he also would hit these shots very low because the clubface was shut at the instant of impact.

For a long time, Hogan worked on a move that he believed would "delay" the closing of the clubface. In fact, this move is very prominently illustrated in his first instruction book, *Power Golf.* What Hogan tried to do, as his hands and arms were about to enter the hitting zone, was to get his right elbow well in front of his hands and the club. When Hogan jerked his right elbow forward so that it was in front of his right hip, his hands and the club would be way behind, and his clubface would be in a wide-open position.

Hogan figured that the more he could keep his right elbow in front, the more he could keep the clubface open, and if he could keep the clubface open as long as possible before impact, he wouldn't hook the ball. If you think about this, it seems like a very logical conclusion. And Hogan was nothing if he was not a very analytic, intelligent individual. But something was wrong. Despite his careful analysis, and despite the fact that he had gained some success as a professional, Hogan was still plagued at times by an uncontrollable hook. And it seems as though the more he tried to keep the clubface open by keeping that right elbow out front, the more he ended up hooking. Can you guess what was wrong?

If you can't, don't berate yourself. You're far from alone. For many years I tried to become a great player too, and I played the PGA Tour from 1968 through 1973. Golf was my life's work, and I could not figure out how to stop a hook either because I had fallen into the same trap in reasoning that Hogan had. And the same has been true for countless other serious players and golf instructors.

Hogan Discovers His "Secret"

72

What was happening in Hogan's swing was this: The more Hogan kept his right elbow leading the hands and club, the more open the face was at impact. However, at some point, Hogan simply had to release his hands and wrists, turning them over in a counterclockwise manner. He had no choice. If he didn't eventually make this release, the clubface would never square up to the back of the ball. So Hogan released. And when he did release, the clubface would move from a completely open position in relation to the swing plane to a completely shut position just after impact. The farther he moved his right elbow down and in front of his right hip, the longer the clubface stayed open and the more violent was the release. The speed of this closing action of the clubface was blindingly fast, and it occurred over a very short distance along the plane of the swing, the impact zone. This clubface release was so fast that it could not be controlled. Sometimes Hogan would make impact with the face dead square, and he'd hit a perfect shot. Occasionally the release would be late, in which case the face would be a little open. Since Hogan's swing path was coming into the ball from the inside, this would result in a shot that was pushed or blocked to the right. But the more frequent error was that the clubface closed a little too quickly: When this happened, Hogan's inside-out swing path plus the closed face would result in tremendous right-to-left spin on the ball, and the big hook.

So once more, Ben Hogan went into his mental lab, so to speak, to analyze his action, and he eventually found his secret. And let me tell you right now, it wasn't some of the things you might have heard about the weaker grip, or getting the club shaft laid off at the top, or keeping the left wrist leading through impact. It was this: Hogan finally asked himself, "What would happen if I got the clubface as open as possible in the backswing and then released the clubface *early* in the downswing instead of releasing it late? What if I got the clubface square in relation to the plane of the swing early, and then simply turned through impact?" So Hogan went to the practice tee and tried it. Instead of pushing that right elbow in front of his hip, almost simultaneously with his two-move that we've discussed, he turned his left forearm counterclockwise at the start of his downswing. This move caused his right forearm to drop and rotate so that the right elbow now stayed up and behind him and the hands dropped down very close to the right hip. Now Hogan's clubface became square to the plane of his swing at or just below waist height. This early hitting with the right forearm often led him to remark that he hit so hard with the right hand/arm that he wished he had two or three of them.

With the left forearm turning and the right forearm dropping the hands down close to the right hip, the handle of the club was positioned on the inner

73

Photo 4.20 Hogan's later career one-plane correction of the right elbow position, now up and on the right side with the club shaft on plane

circle and the clubhead square to the plane on the outer circle. This position, illustrated beautifully in later photographs of Hogan and, in particular, in photographs by Jules Alexander in the book *The Hogan Mystique*, when compared to the photographs in *Power Golf*, illustrates the dramatic difference in his swing. Once Hogan had started the downswing in a manner that immediately put his hands on the inner circle, the clubface on the outer circle and square to the plane, all he had to do was to keep turning his torso freely and move the hands around, tight to the body, to the left on the inner circle to complete the in-to-in arc. As a result, the clubface would automatically be moving square to the arc throughout impact, as long as he kept his arms swinging around to the left. So Ben Hogan did have a secret, and it was that instead of delaying the rotation of the clubface by shoving his right elbow down and forward and playing golf from wide open to closed during impact, he dropped his right forearm and released or rotated his forearm and club early in the downswing. This did three things for him: It dropped his hands down onto the inner circle, it brought the club out in front of him onto the outer circle, and it squared the clubface to the plane of the swing. There was no longer any violent release or closing of the clubface that had to be timed perfectly at impact.

You can see ample evidence that Hogan used this method by viewing down-target photographs of his post-impact position in his later competitive years. Let's backtrack for a moment to see this evidence. Do you remember how I stated that when the club shaft is halfway down on the backswing, in order to be perfectly square to the swing plane, the clubface should not be pointing straight up? Instead, the toe of the club should be pointing about just to the right of straight up? Well, if you are simply turning your torso and your arms through the impact zone, you should see close to a mirror image, approximately the same squareness of the clubface to the swing plane, at a point halfway into the follow-through. That is to say that at this point past impact, the toe of the club should most definitely not be rotated to where the clubface is turned over to the left.

Instead, the club's toe should be either toe up (slightly closed to the plane due to the club's speed) or again be pointing slightly to the right of directly upward, or toward about 45 degrees (perfectly square). This is the position in which the clubface is still somewhat square (or only slightly closed) to the plane that it is

Photo 4.21 One-plane clubface rotated shut in follow-through

Photo 4.22 One-plane clubface square to the plane

traveling along. Look carefully at photos of Hogan in this position (preferably when hitting a longer iron so that the position of the clubface is less distorted by the loft on the club). The toe of Hogan's club pointed pretty much straight up. Now from this position to the finish, the clubface rolls over in a closing motion, which is the mirror image of the second half of the backswing, where (as we have discussed) the clubface rolls open to the plane.

Why is it that Hogan never directly revealed this secret? We'll never know for certain. I have it on excellent authority that at one time, well after his playing career had ended, Hogan had tentatively agreed to do a story with a major golfing publication in which he would reveal his secret. For whatever reason, Hogan ended up backing out on doing this. I believe that Hogan simply decided that future golfers should pretty much figure this out for themselves.

However, Hogan did leave us some clues. (I'll bet it amused him to see if anyone could pick up on them.) The best clue of all was when he stated that after trying for so long to play golf from an open clubface position to a closed clubface position, he had finally realized that he needed to play from "shut to open."

Now, what did Hogan mean by this? Well, what he meant was that in the first half of the downswing, his left forearm rotation and right forearm drop served to put the clubhead into what felt and was assumed to be a shut position midway in the downswing. As I have already described in detail, the position of Hogan's clubface was actually dead square to the plane of his swing at this point, but no one except Hogan had really figured that out yet. So, by the definitions of his day, Hogan had the clubface in a shut position halfway down. Then, when Hogan rotated his body, his arms, and the club through and past impact around to the left to where the shaft was level with the ground and pointing to the target, the toe of the club was again pointing slightly to the right of a straight-up position. By the definitions of his day, Hogan now had a clubface that was open after impact. But as we have seen, Hogan's clubface was again, in truth, square in relation to the plane of his swing.

Now that I have fully explained Hogan's secret, let's get back to where we left off. From this halfway point in the downswing, you will continue to turn your body through impact to the end of the swing. As your arms approach impact, your left arm will start moving across your chest to the left while your right forearm releases the club on plane through impact to the finish. Your left elbow will bend as you pull it backward and upward so that it reaches your left shirt seam or goes slightly beyond it.

Golfers with strong grips and closed clubfaces will not need to rotate the left forearm much to keep the clubface square as they move around the inner circle. Those with

Photo 4.23 One-plane left elbow moving up and back in follow-through

neutral to weak grips and square to open clubfaces will need to continue to rotate the left arm counterclockwise while they go around on the inner circle. A good rule of thumb for these square or open-face players is to turn the left forearm hard to the finish and keep the handle moving around to the left. If you are hooking, you are turning the left forearm okay but are either stopping the handle or are not moving it around enough to the left. Conversely, if you are fading too much, you are probably moving the handle around to the left but have insufficient left forearm rotation. If you are doing both, straight shots are the order of the day. Concurrently to the forearm action, of course, you have been turning your shoulders and trunk around your spine and toward the target. This turning of your body should be as full, as fast, and as vigorous as you can make it. Remember, as long as your clubface is moving along your plane line and is square to your plane line, you can turn just as hard as you want.

If anything, I have noticed that some golfers who try to develop a one-plane swing tend to be a little tentative through the impact zone. They think that they may need to do something through the impact zone to make sure the ball flies straight. All you need know is this fact: Once you've ingrained the aforementioned principles of the one-plane swing, just keep turning your body and firing your arms around to the left aggressively, almost carelessly and sloppily, through impact to hit it as hard as you want.

To complete a description of what happens here: Your right elbow will remain up and behind you until just before impact. Then, in reaction to the strong hitting motion of your right forearm, the right arm will gradually straighten and be thrown across your torso. Let me emphasize, you need merely to be hitting with the right forearm and allowing your left arm to move back and up as described, rotate the left arm appropriate to your grip, and turn your torso fully and freely.

Beyond impact, the right arm will continue to straighten and your right wrist will throw (the left wrist will cup backward). This throwing action of the right wrist will throw the club shaft up the plane to the left.

There should be very little counterclockwise rotation of the right forearm until you're beyond waist high, the point where the shaft is pointing to your target. (Remember your key checkpoint: When the shaft is parallel to the ground beyond impact, the toe of the clubhead should be pointing toe-up or slightly

Photo 4.24 One-plane right forearm and wrist throw up the plane just beyond impact

right of toe-up.) When your hands are at about waist height, your right wrist and forearm will begin to rotate naturally, throwing the club shaft up the swing plane to the completion of the follow-through.

There you have it—the completed one-plane downswing. While I firmly believe that any reasonably athletic golfer can successfully develop this swing, naturally, many will encounter pitfalls along the way. Let's discuss what these are most likely to be and how to solve them.

LESSON: The Right Elbow Leading and the Club Getting Stuck Behind the Body

This is the classic problem that many would-be one-plane golfers have: Halfway into the downswing, the right elbow is in front of the right hip. This is the position that Ben Hogan played from for much of his career, and which many teachers still try to get their students to emulate. No wonder so many golfers, particularly serious golfers who practice and take lessons often, struggle with it.

Photo 4.25 One-plane right elbow leading and club stuck behind

When the right elbow is in this position, the left arm, instead of staying pinned to the chest, must necessarily pull up and away from the chest. The hands and the clubhead are left way behind, so the clubhead must swing on a path that's from too far inside the ball, while the clubface is wide open in relation to the swing path.

From the halfway point in the downswing, in order to contact the ball at all the player must rotate the fore-arms and wrists very rapidly in order to release the clubhead back into the ball. The result will be a very inside-out swing path at impact. And this in turn means shots that either are pushed to the right or badly hooked; shots that are hit either fat or thin, depending on whether the shallow plane contacts the ground behind the ball or does not contact it at all; and shallow topped shots. In extreme cases where the golfer's manual attempt to square up the clubface is very late, shanking can also very easily occur.

If you've read my story about Ben Hogan carefully, you should already know the key to correcting these faults: Your arms must swing around your body while your torso is simultaneously turning around your spine. At the start of the downswing, as your body is rotating, your right elbow should remain up and behind you. The counterclockwise rotation of the left forearm and your right forearm drop will ensure that your hands are moving along the inner circle, while the clubhead is also on plane and square to the plane, moving along the outer circle.

As your body continues turning, your right forearm releases the club on plane into and through impact while your left arm continues to bend and to pull itself up and behind you, toward the seam on the left side of your shirt. Just prior to impact, the right arm will start to straighten as it is thrown across your body. Through impact, your left elbow continues moving up and back until it has reached or even gone past your left side shirtsleeve; meanwhile your right arm continues to straighten and move around your body on the inner circle to the left with no conscious rotation. When the hands are about at waist height after impact the right wrist and forearm finally begin to rotate over the left, and the left wrist will be bent backward (due to the right wrist throw just after impact) as the club shaft is thrown up the final portion of the swing plane.

Once again, all of the preceding points will fall into place if, from the top, you correctly and continuously turn your torso around your spine while dropping and releasing your right forearm to get your hands on the inner circle and the clubface back to square with your swing plane.

A number of the drills described in Chapter 5 will aid you in correcting the right elbow leading/club stuck behind problem. They are as follows: the Arms Around Body Drill (Variation 3); the X Drill (Variation 2); the Close the A Drill (Variation 2); the One-Plane Release Drill, which was also outlined in *The Plane Truth for Golfers*; the Palm Around/ Spine Over Drill; the Right Arm Pointer Drill (Variation 2); the Right Hand Throw Drill; and the Elbows Back Drill.

Photo 4.26 One-plane right wrist and forearm throwing club shaft up the plane

Fact Versus Feel

If you have been playing from a position in which your right elbow is leading the downswing, and then you make all the correct movements I've described, there's no doubt that your downswing will feel incredibly different. The swinging of your arms will **feel** extremely tight and cramped. That's fine. If past impact you are extending your right arm directly above (in line with) the lower-left section of the X in the X Drill, your arms are in the right place. It should **feel** like you are *throwing* the club down and around with your right forearm right from the start of the downswing.

It will also **feel** like your arms are moving on a virtually flat plane, like a merry-go-round, and that they're moving low around your belt. This, too, is fine. I joke with my students that they should feel like their hands are going to get "belt burn" from moving so low around the body.

It should **feel** as though your arms are not acting independently, but rather that they are tied in to your body turn. Meanwhile, as the club is moving it should have a very lively, whipping feel. And past impact, you should **feel** as if your hands and arms are turned impossibly far around you and to your left. Even though they feel this way, they are still moving on the correct plane.

I'd like to add here that I think it's a very good idea, while practicing your new downswing on the range, to intermingle the Arms Around Body Drill (both backswing and downswing variations) with the actual practice shots. If you do this, I guarantee that you will **feel** as if you're hitting the ball with incredibly short arms, or "gator arms," which is a very vivid image. That's okay. Just know that your arms are functioning correctly and they will allow the clubhead to extend down to where its face meets the ball squarely and solidly.

81

LESSON: Fixing the Fault of the Arms Disconnecting from the Body

Here we have the golfer who struggles with a slightly different right arm problem from the golfer who gets the right elbow in front of the body. In this case, the player's right elbow does not move in front of the right hip. Rather, the player throws the entire right arm out away from the right aide. Concurrent with and because of this disconnection of the right elbow from the body, the

Photo 4.27 One-plane fault of arms thrown too far in front of the body

Photo 4.28 One-plane steep and outside-in downswing

player's upper left arm moves out away from the chest and the hands and club are thrown well outside the plane that they swung back on.

As you can probably guess, the player with this problem will bring the clubhead down to the ball on a very steep plane, and one that is moving down from outside the target line. The usual results: Fat, popped-up shots, steep tops in which the descending clubhead meets the top of the ball, shots pulled straight to the left, or big left-to-right slices. Very steep divots are also this player's dubious trademark.

If you suffer from this outside-in downswing, the key to correcting it is to improve the movement of your right forearm at the very start of the downswing. Try to keep your right elbow in the position it was in as you reached the top; in other words, keep it up and behind you, while you lower your right forearm (and

Photo 4.29 One-plane downswing with right elbow still up and behind the right side and a correct forearm drop very near the right pant pocket

your left arm with it, since both hands are holding the club). Lowering your right forearm while keeping the right elbow up and behind instead of throwing them outward will put your hands on the inner circle very close to a spot just below your right pant pocket.

A split second after you drop your right forearm, as you enter impact, start to bend your left elbow and begin pulling your left elbow to the left, keeping it tight against your chest. Continue pulling the left elbow toward the seam of your shirt on your left side. You must keep that left elbow moving to or beyond that seam all the way through impact and into the follow-through. If you drop your right forearm down and move your left elbow as I've described, your left arm cannot help but stay in tight to your chest as it is pulled across your body in the direction of the target. If you have a weak to neutral grip, you will want to rotate the left forearm as it moves around the body. As your left elbow keeps pulling behind you, the right arm, as a result of the throwing release of the right forearm, will automatically straighten out a short distance beyond impact. At this point about halfway into the follow-through, the right hand should throw the club shaft up the plane as we have discussed, and finally, the right hand will roll over the left as the hands move up to the finish position.

Once you have corrected the faulty movements in both arms, the clubhead will move from inside the line coming down, to squarely on line at impact, then rapidly back to the inside beyond impact and into the follow-through. When you do this, your steep, outside-in downswing will disappear. You may find that you will overdo these corrections a little bit, so that you start hitting a right-to-left draw or a slight hook. If so, don't be alarmed. As I've said, you may need to overcorrect for a while just to be certain you have rid yourself of the faulty arm movements. You can easily straighten that hook out by emphasizing moving the club's handle around on the inner circle to the left. As mentioned earlier, the more you move and the faster you move the hands around on the inner circle to the left, the more you will fade the ball. The more you rotate the left forearm and the less or more slowly you move the handle around the inner circle, the more you will hook or pull.

Following in Chapter 5 are several drills to help you stop throwing the arms and club outside the plane line as you start down: the Towel Drill; the Arms Around Body Drill (Variation 3); the Glove Under Arm Drill; and the X Drill (Variation 2).

84

Fact Versus Feel

Similarly to the player who had the right elbow leading the club in the downswing, the player who habitually throws the arms and the club outside the plane at the start of the downswing will **feel** like the arms are now in a very cramped position on the downswing. The left arm will feel like it is in too close to the body, and the right hand will feel like it is almost inside the right pant pocket. But what feels cramped really means that you're simply moving your hands along the inner circle, which allows the club to move correctly along the outer circle (on-plane). Just make sure that as you pull your left elbow up and back, your left forearm is moving at that 45-degree angle to the left of your target line, as indicated by the lower-left line of the crossed clubs as mentioned in the X Drill.

At the point of impact, you will probably also **feel** as though your arms are too far behind your body. The reason you have this sensation is that your hips are turning but your right hand is near your right hip instead of being thrown way out in front of it. Thus it feels as though your hands are behind you. Keep making the downswing moves we have discussed, along with the various drills to help ingrain the correct positions, and you'll quickly become accustomed to this hands-behind-body position.

Also, just beyond impact, you may well **feel** as though your club shaft is swinging on a plane that is much too flat, that the clubhead is coming around rather than swinging so violently down during impact. That's true for just about every handicap golfer, mainly because most golfers have been taught to keep the club moving along the target line, or to "extend." Of course, you by now understand that if the club stays on or near the target line after impact, it is moving on a straight line and that is off-plane. You might ask, "How can I possibly be extending when my left arm is bent and so far to my left halfway into the follow-through?" The answer is that beyond impact, it is your right arm that extends the club along the plane line. As long as your right arm is fully extended when that arm and the club shaft are parallel to the ground halfway into the follow-through, you have achieved correct and full extension—even though your left arm is bent and tucked close to your side.

For a while, you will have to trust the one-plane action, and this particular sensation of the clubhead coming around after impact is a part of what you have to trust, even if it makes you wonder how the ball is going to go straight. Let me reassure you, the more correctly you assimilate the technique described in this chapter, the straighter the flight of your shots will become. Moreover, when you see the golf ball take off toward the target like a bullet often enough, your worries about the clubhead coming too far inside will quickly vanish.

To sum up, I realize full well that I have given you a lot to digest about the one-plane golf swing. I don't expect anyone to simply read my instructions and immediately execute this swing method anything near perfectly. I urge you to work on getting the one-plane setup correct first. Practice it often in front of a mirror until it feels like second nature. Then and only then should you start working on the various movements of the one-plane backswing; and then, once you have confidence that you've assimilated the backswing movements, you can move on to the one-plane downswing. Use a mirror often as you work on the various movements within the swing.

I urge you to be patient and take it one step at a time. You may find that when you are part of the way but not all the way toward assimilating the one-plane golf swing, you are hitting some bad shots, shots that do not fit the pattern of your previous swing errors. If so, fix your faults by working hard on the practice drills in the following chapter.

One-Plane Drills

This chapter contains descriptions of drills that will help you integrate the feels of the one-plane golf swing. The drills are grouped according to the particular swing problems they help to correct. (Several drills that are beneficial to both one-plane and two-plane golfers are listed both here and in Chapter 9.)

I believe drills are vital in communicating the exact feels for making correct moves in the golf swing. Some drills are designed to give a better understanding of the entire swing. Other drills isolate a particular movement within the swing. Those isolated drills are not the entire swing but simply highlight a segment of the motion, and when learned, that segment is inserted back into the full swing. This is much like a mechanic who takes out a faulty engine, repairs it, and then reinstalls it. The isolated part is better repaired when removed from the whole and then replaced. Regardless of whether the drills are for isolated parts of the swing or for a full swing correction, try every drill that relates to each particular lesson that applies to your game. Your understanding of the correction you need to make will be greatly enhanced.

Photo 5.1 Club Across Shoulders Drill (Variation 1): Shoulder turn in the zone

Fault: Reverse Pivot on Backswing

88

Club Across Shoulders Drill (Variation 1)

Hold a club across the front of your shoulders and assume your address position for the one-plane swing. Turn your shoulders fully, so that the club shaft points to the right of the ball and toward the outer half (the outside 24 inches) of the zone that runs from the ball to 48 inches outside the ball.

As you make this turn, your spine and head should drift slightly to the right (away from the target). Check in a mirror to see that this slight drift occurs. Return to address position and repeat several times.

Photo 5.2 Club Across Shoulders Drill (Variation 1): Shoulder turn in the zone and behind the ball

Wallet Pocket Left Drill

Assume the one-plane address position. Have a friend stand behind you and hold a club horizontal to the ground at hip height, with the grip just lightly touching the outside edge of your left hip.

Make a full turn with your upper body. As you make this turn, your left wallet pocket should stay in contact with the shaft through the completion of the backswing.

As an alternate to having a friend holding a club, you can perform the drill by sticking a golf shaft in the ground so that it's standing vertically with the grip just touching your left hip. Make the same backswing movement so that your left wallet pocket stays in contact with the grip.

Photo 5.3 Wallet Pocket Left Drill: Club shaft just touching left hip at address

Photo 5.4 Wallet Pocket Left Drill: Left hip maintaining contact with the club shaft at top of backswing

Object-in-the-Sky Drill

This drill was invented by Peter Jacobsen, and it presents a vivid image. Stand in the one-plane address position and imagine that an object such as an airplane or a blimp is in the air directly behind and above you.

Execute your backswing turn, making certain that you turn your entire chest to the right. At the top of the backswing, turn your head to the right. You should be in a position where you can see the object out of the corner of your right eye.

Repeat several times. This drill reminds you to turn your entire chest, not just the shoulders as many players do. Now, from the top of the backswing, turn 180 degrees through impact, keeping your turn in the zone all the way to the finish of the swing. Your shoulders and hips should be facing the target, and you should still have some forward bend toward the zone in your spine. Turn your head to the left. You should be in a position where you can see the object out of the corner of your left eye.

Photo 5.5 Object-in-the-Sky Drill: Overhead object in the sky at address

Photo 5.6 Object-in-the-Sky Drill: Turn entire chest in backswing until you can see the object.

Photo 5.7 Object-in-the-Sky Drill: Turn entire chest around into the follow-through until you can see the object.

Photo 5.8 Club Across Shoulders Drill (Variation 2): Shoulder turn into the inner portion of the zone

Fault: Too-Shallow Shoulder Turn on Backswing

Club Across Shoulders Drill (Variation 2)

Hold a club across the front of your shoulders and assume your address position for the one-plane swing. Turn your shoulders fully, on an angle so that the club shaft points even with the ball and toward the inner half (the inside 24 inches) of the zone that runs from the ball to 48 inches outside the ball.

As you make this turn, your head and spine should drift slightly to the left (toward the target).

Check in a mirror to see that this slight drift occurs. Return to address position and repeat several times.

Photo 5.9 Club Across Shoulders Drill (Variation 2): Steep shoulder turn with slight spine tilt left

Photo 5.10 Arms Around Body Drill (Variation 1): Erect posture and club shaft held out parallel to the ground

Fault: Arms in Front of Body on Backswing

Arms Around Body Drill (Variation 1)

Standing upright, grip a club with your arms out in front of you at chest height, with the club shaft parallel to the ground.

Without turning your chest, pull your right elbow briskly behind you; the elbow should move backward at a 45-degree angle. Your left arm should be pulled straight across your chest by this right arm movement, and the club shaft should now point directly to your right.

Repeat as often as necessary to ingrain the correct arm movements.

Photo 5.11 Arms Around Body Drill (Variation 1): Move right elbow back and pull left arm across chest without turning upper body.

Bucket Drill

Get a small pail or a range-ball bucket. Assume the one-plane address position, holding the sides of the bucket instead of a club. The opening of the bucket should be facing on a 45-degree angle up and away from you.

Make your start-of-backswing right arm movement as in the Arms Around Body Drill described previously. At the halfway point going back (hands at hip height), the opening of the bucket (which represents the clubhead) should be pointing at a 45-degree angle to your right. (If it were to point directly to your right, away from the target, it would show that you have rotated the club well open in relation to your swing plane.)

Next, pull your left elbow back, up, and around your left side, pulling your right arm, your hands, and the bucket around with it. At this point halfway into the follow-through, the bucket should again face at the same 45-degree angle away from you. (If the bucket faces directly away from you to the left, it means you have rotated the clubface closed too quickly after impact.)

Practice your right arm and left arm movements repeatedly while holding the bucket, to get the feel of the clubhead moving through the impact zone with no rotation.

Photo 5.12 Bucket Drill: Hold the pail at address on a 45-degree angle.

Photo 5.13 Bucket Drill: Pail is still at 45-degree angle at backswing midpoint.

Photo 5.14 Bucket Drill: Midpoint follow-through should mirror midpoint backswing.

Club Set Drill

From the one-plane address position, draw the club back from the ball, as discussed in Chapter 3, to the halfway-back position in the backswing. At this point, take your left hand off the club shaft.

Now, using your right hand and arm only, rotate your wrist and move your forearm up and back to take the club shaft around and up to the top, while making certain that the right elbow continues moving back and upward, never forward.

Once you've gotten the club to the top, reach up and around with your left hand and arm, replacing it on the grip. Be careful while reaching up and back with the left hand that you do not raise your spine or your left shoulder.

Notice how far the left arm must move and how it rotates with the back of the forearm moving up in order to regrip the club. This drill teaches you how both arms move to set the club at the top of the backswing.

Photo 5.15 Club Set Drill: Go to backswing midpoint and remove the left hand.

Photo 5.16 Club Set Drill: Move to top of backswing with only right arm.

Photo 5.17 Club Set Drill: Stretch your left arm across and grip the club at the top of backswing.

X Drill (Variation 1)

Place two clubs on the ground in front of where you will take your stance, so that they form a big letter X. If you were to play an actual shot, the ball would be at the center of this X. Assume your stance for the one-plane swing with the club just behind where the ball would be.

On the first half of your backswing, draw your right elbow back and up. The movement of your right elbow should be along the same plane line as the bottom-right segment of the X.

From this point in the backswing, as your right elbow continues up and back, allow the right forearm to rotate. Your left arm, which has been pulled tight across your chest, should now also rotate around and up to the top of the backswing along the same plane line as the bottom-right segment of the X.

Practice this backswing portion of the X Drill repeatedly to keep the motion of both arms correct.

Photo 5.18 X Drill (Variation 1): At address with club shafts forming an X

Photo 5.19 X Drill (Variation 1): Right elbow moves up and back along the leg of the X in first half of backswing.

Photo 5.20 X Drill (Variation 1): Left arm at top of backswing extends on leg of the X.

Glove Under Arm Drill

This is a drill that Scott McCarron uses a lot. Place a golf glove (or other small, pliable object like a clubhead cover) underneath your left arm so your upper left arm holds it against the chest.

Using what you have learned about the backswing, take a three-quarter length backswing while keeping the glove secured between upper left arm and chest. Make a series of these three-quarter backswings and see if you can continue to hold the glove in place.

After you have gained command of the backswing motion, do the drill completely by making a three-quarter backswing, then a three-quarter downswing, while keeping the glove trapped between your upper left arm and chest. In the downswing, you will pull the glove across the chest and around it to the left.

Repeat often.

Photo 5.21 Glove Under Arm Drill: Club cover under left arm at address

Photo 5.22 Glove Under Arm Drill: Club cover still pinned under left arm at top of backswing

Photo 5.23 Glove Under Arm Drill: Club cover still pinned just past midpoint of follow-through

Right Arm Pointer Drill (Variation 1)

Hold the club as you normally would in the one-plane address position, then remove your left hand from the club. With your right hand and arm, draw the handle back just a bit while leaving the clubhead behind the ball. Move the handle just enough so that the club shaft and your right forearm form a straight line.

Then make your right-elbow-up-and-back movement. Notice how the clubface remains more or less in front of you. Notice also that the clubface is still pointing toward the target line (as opposed to being whipped around behind you).

This simple move is the Right Arm Pointer. Repeat it often to get the feel of this first slight move in the take-away that gets everything started correctly. After making this move a number of times, continue back by cocking the club

Photo 5.24 Right Arm Pointer Drill (Variation 1): Club shaft and right arm form a straight line.

Photo 5.25 Right Arm Pointer Drill (Variation 1): While right elbow moves, keep club shaft pointing toward the target line.

Photo 5.26 Right Arm Pointer Drill (Variation 1): Correct top of backswing with only the right arm.

Photo 5.27 Right Arm Pointer Drill (Variation 1): Bring your left arm across and up to grip the club with both hands.

upward and backward by rotating your right wrist and forearm, then bring your left arm up so your hand meets the grip and you're in the completed backswing position.

I might add that the Right Arm Pointer Drill was very helpful to Olin Browne, who at age 46 finished 23rd on the PGA Tour money list in 2005. This drill taught Olin how to eliminate his tendency to allow the clubhead to move too far inside, behind his arms and too low to the ground at the start of the backswing.

Close the A Drill (Variation 1)

This drill trains you to make the correct movement with your right elbow up and back on the backswing. Imagine that at the address position, when viewed from a down-target position, your right upper arm and the seam on the right side of your shirt are the sides of a capital A, with the top of that letter A being your shoulder joint.

With both hands on the club, make the up-and-back move with your right elbow that we've discussed in Chapter 3. Imagine that your right upper arm is going to close that letter A by moving back until it reaches the seam of your shirt, or even goes a little behind the seam. If you can close the A, you'll have made the correct initial move of the backswing, and you'll also see how in response your left arm has automatically been pulled tight across your body.

Be careful you don't over-turn your body, especially your hips, while trying to close the A as all you will be doing is chasing the shirt seam around instead of catching it. Sequence should be as follows: only a slight turn of the upper torso as you close the A, then complete the entire turn.

Photo 5.28 Close the A Drill (Variation 1): The A at address

Photo 5.29 Close the A Drill (Variation 1): Closing the A

Fault: Swinging the Club Inside Too Quickly on Backswing

X Drill (Variation 1)
This drill is described on page 95.

Club Set Drill
This drill is described on page 94.

Right Arm Pointer Drill (Variation 1)
This drill is described on page 97.

Fault: Raising the Spine Angle and Thrusting the Hips on Downswing

Arms Around Body Drill (Variation 2)

Stand upright without holding a club. Instead, cross the fingers of both hands together and hold your arms out so the palms are together and your thumbs point straight up. Bend forward from the hips to assume your one-plane address position. Your thumbs should point upward and outward about 40 degrees, at the same angle as your spine.

Now make the same movements as in Variation 1 of the Arms Around Body Drill (see page 92). That is, pull your right elbow backward and

Photo 5.30 Arms Around Body Drill (Variation 2): At address with thumbs pointed upward and outward

upward and extend your left arm across your chest for the backswing, while keeping your thumbs pointed upward and outward.

Then pull your left elbow backward and upward and extend your right arm across your chest for the forward swing. Keep your thumbs pointed upward and outward.

Try holding your upper body as quiet as possible and just move the arms, checking to make sure that your thumbs point somewhat upward and outward. (Remember, the thumbs started at the same angle as the spine. So if your thumbs don't stay angled the same throughout the movement, but rather point straight up, it means you are overrotating your forearms.) Repeat as often as necessary to feel sure you are maintaining your spine angle.

Photo 5.31 Arms Around Body Drill (Variation 2): Right elbow back and up, left arm across, thumbs pointed upward and outward

Photo 5.32 Arms Around Body Drill (Variation 2): Left elbow back and up, right arm across, thumbs pointed upward and outward

Club Across Shoulders Drill (Variation 3)

Hold a club across the front of your shoulders and assume your address position for the one-plane swing. Turn your shoulders to the top of the backswing

Next, turn your shoulders through the impact zone to a point where the club across your shoulders is pointing back toward the middle of the zone. (It's helpful if you can have a partner present to verify that the club shaft is pointing within the limits of the zone as it should.)

As you continue turning to the finish, allow your spine to come up slightly and your shoulders to point to the outside edge of the zone. As you do, lift your right or rear foot off the ground. You should be able to stay balanced with all your weight on your left leg. Return to address position and repeat several times.

Photo 5.33 Club Across Shoulders Drill (Variation 3): Club points into zone on backswing.

Photo 5.34 Club Across Shoulders Drill (Variation 3): Club points into zone on follow-through.

Brute Drill

The name of this drill, from Peter Jacobsen, is taken from the trade name for a large plastic garbage container. Here's the drill: Get a large cylindrical object, large enough so that it can fit over your upper torso. (If this cylinder is indeed a garbage container, you would need to cut the bottom off it about 15 to 18 inches from the top to fit inside.) Cross your arms in front of your chest and hold the opposite shoulders. Then have a friend place the cylinder over your upper torso. Bend over approximately 35 to 45 degrees.

Now, while your friend holds the "Brute" in place, as still as possible, turn your torso to the top of the backswing. Hold for a second, and then turn your torso through the downswing and into a full finish position.

Notice that to make the downswing upper body turn successfully, you must transfer your weight onto your left or forward foot. As long as you're being held captive within the cylinder, go ahead and repeat the drill 10 to 12 times, feeling your weight totally on your forward foot during the downswing.

Photo 5.35 Brute Drill: At a bent-over address position in the "Brute"

Photo 5.36 Brute Drill: Correct backswing turn in the "Brute"

Photo 5.37 Brute Drill: Correct follow-through turn with the weight on the left leg

Object-in-the-Sky Drill

This drill is described on page 90.

Fault: Curing Loss of Spine Angle, Hip Turn Backing Up, and Outside-In Downswing

Brute Drill

This drill is described on page 103.

Club Across Shoulders Drill (Variation 3)

This drill is described on page 102.

Arms Around Body Drill (Variation 2)

This drill is described on page 100.

Fault: Alleviating Lateral Hip Slide and Shoulder Tilt Problems on Downswing

Anti-Hook Grip
Pressure Drill

Find a very small object like a BB, a small pellet, a twig, or even a hard kernel of corn. Put your left hand on the grip, holding the club up so that the base of your left thumb is parallel to the ground. Place the small object just behind the second knuckle on your left thumb. Then carefully take your right hand grip so that the base of your right thumb covers the object and holds it in place.

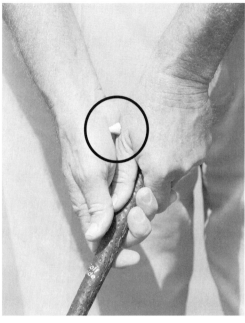

Photo 5.38 Anti-Hook Grip Pressure Drill: Squeeze an object between the right palm heel pad and the base of the left thumb.

Now take some practice swings. As you swing down through impact, increase the pressure with the heel of your right palm on the object, never allowing it to slip out. When you are consistently adding pressure and holding the object in place, you can try this drill on the practice range while hitting actual shots.

Brute Drill
This drill is described on page 103.

Arms Around Body Drill (Variation 2)
This drill is described on page 100.

Object-in-the-Sky Drill
This drill is described on page 90.

Photo 5.39 Arms Around Body Drill (Variation 3): Erect posture and club shaft held out parallel to ground

Fault: Right Elbow Leading/Club Stuck Behind on Downswing

106

Arms Around Body Drill (Variation 3)

Stand upright while holding a club out in front of you at chest height, with the club shaft parallel to the ground and the toe of the clubhead pointed straight up.

Without turning your chest, pull your left elbow briskly behind you, with the elbow moving backward at a 45-degree angle. Your right arm should be pulled across your chest by this left arm movement, and the club shaft should point directly to your left with the toe pointed straight up.

Repeat as often as necessary to ingrain the correct arm movements.

Photo 5.40 Arms Around Body Drill (Variation 3): Move the left elbow back, the right arm across the chest without turning the upper body.

X Drill (Variation 2)

Place two clubs on the ground in front of you so that they form a letter X, as in the first X Drill variation. Assume your top-of-backswing position. Make your downswing movement in slow motion. Just before impact, start drawing your left elbow back and up toward the seam on your shirt and your right forearm to about waist high in the follow-through.

As your left arm continues back, your right arm, which has been thrown across your chest, should now rotate up and around into the follow-through along the same plane line as the bottom-left segment of the X.

Practice this downswing portion of the X Drill repeatedly to keep the motion of both arms correct.

Photo 5.41 X Drill (Variation 2): Left elbow moves up and back along the leg of the X in first half of follow-through.

Photo 5.42 X Drill (Variation 2): Right arm at finish extends on leg of the X.

Close the A Drill (Variation 2)

This drill teaches you to make the correct movement with your left elbow up and back on the downswing. Imagine that in a position just before impact, when viewed from an up-target position, your left upper arm and the seam on the left side of your shirt are the sides of a capital A, with your shoulder joint being the top or joining point of that A.

With both hands on the club, make a vigorous movement with your left elbow as we've discussed for the downswing. Make your left upper arm "close the A" by moving back until it reaches your shirt seam, or even goes slightly past it. If you make this move correctly, you'll see that your right arm will automatically be thrown across your chest.

Photo 5.43 Close the A Drill (Variation 2): The A as viewed from the target at impact

Photo 5.44 Close the A Drill (Variation 2): Close the A in the follow-through by pulling the left elbow up and back and the right arm across.

One-Plane Release Drill

Without a club, bend your spine forward and place your hands, as if holding a club, opposite your right side. Imagine that about one-half of a circle extends from behind your right foot, around in front of your feet, and then back around your left foot. This is what I've referred to in *The Plane Truth for Golfers* as the "inner circle." Practice moving your hands from right to left in front of you directly above this inner circle, making sure that you keep your hands and wrists very firm as you do so. This is the path your hands should move along through the impact zone.

Next, take an iron club and set up in the address position. Move your hands back along the inner circle until your hands are behind you on your right and your right elbow is behind your right hip. Then turn your body counterclockwise through the hitting zone to just short of impact.

From here, let your left upper arm move upward and backward toward the seam of your shirt on the left side as your right arm starts to release across your torso and your hands continue moving along the inner circle to the left.

Repeat this movement of the hands and arms back from and then through the ball's position, this time taking note of the movement of the clubhead. It should move around an arc on the ground that is also a half circle, one that forms its arc about 18 inches outside the inner circle and

Photo 5.45 One-Plane Release Drill: On the inner and outer circle entering impact area

Photo 5.46 One-Plane Release Drill: Turning and moving the arms on the inner and outer circles to impact

Photo 5.47 One-Plane Release Drill: Turning and moving the arms on the inner and outer circles to post-impact

upon which the ball would lie. This is what I referred to as the "outer circle" in *The Plane Truth for Golfers*. Remember that the clubface should remain fairly square to the arc of the outer circle throughout its back-and-forth movement above it. For golfers with strong grips and closed clubfaces, very little left arm rotation will be required to keep the clubface square to the arc. Golfers with neutral to weak grips and square to open clubfaces will need to rotate the left forearm somewhat as the handle moves around the inner circle to keep the clubface square to the arc of the outer circle.

Palm Around/Spine Over Drill

You need a partner for this drill. He or she should stand behind you. From the address position and without a club, make your one-plane swing in slow motion. When you reach the midway point in your follow-through, your partner should reach in front of you and grasp your right forearm with his or her left hand. The person should slowly pull your right arm toward him or her while keeping the palm somewhat facing you (the back of your hand will face the target). At the same time, your partner should use his or her other hand to push your back forward and downward to increase your spine angle.

Repeat this drill a number of times. It will instill in you the contrasting movement of the arms and the torso, teaching your arms to move more horizontally, like a merry-go-round, while your torso turn is more vertical, like a Ferris wheel.

Once you have the feel of this drill, you can practice it "live." Out on the practice range, go out and hit easy three-quarter shots with a seven-iron. After impact, try to finish the swing with your right arm well around you, but with the palm facing you (back of hand toward the target). Meanwhile, try to bend your spine slightly forward. This enables you to feel the contrasting forces of your more horizontal arm movement and your more vertical torso turn.

Photo 5.48 Palm Around/Spine Over Drill: As the right arm is pulled around, the left shoulder is pushed into an upright position.

Right Arm Pointer Drill (Variation 2)

Start from your top-of-the-backswing position. Slowly bring the club down until the clubhead reaches the point of impact. With only your right hand on the club, keep moving the handle around so that the club shaft and your right arm form a straight line tight across your chest with the club shaft 90 degrees to the target line.

Repeat several times. Then, at the 90-degree across the chest position, bring your left hand up to meet your right hand on the club's grip. Notice how far around to the left your left elbow must be (at least to the seam of the shirt) to grip the club. This will give you the position of your swing as it nears the finish.

You will only have to lift the arms slightly to be at the end of the swing.

Photo 5.49 Right Arm Pointer Drill (Variation 2): Making a correct follow-through with only the right arm

Photo 5.50 Right Arm Pointer Drill (Variation 2): Place the left hand on the grip and feel the position of the left arm and elbow.

Right Hand Throw Drill

Get a small hula hoop or similar ringlike object that is at least 24 inches in diameter (larger is preferable). Drop it over your head and hold it in your left hand at just above waist height. Bend your spine angle forward about 35 to 40 degrees. Place your right hand so the butt of that hand is on the outside of the hoop, opposite the center of your body, with the palm at 90 degrees to the hoop.

Now move your right hand forward, keeping it square (90 degrees) along the plane of the hoop, through the impact zone and up beyond your left hip. Make sure not to turn your hand or wrist over, just keep it moving along the plane of the hoop, so that when your hand reaches a point opposite your left hip, the palm points up and behind you.

This motion should be just like that of a shortstop throwing the ball across his body to second base for a force-out. Repeat several times. This drill teaches you the correct throwing movement of the right hand and wrist through impact, moving the club up the plane line rather than flipping it over prematurely. The right hand does turn over, but after hip high.

Photo 5.51 Right Hand Throw Drill: Right hand square to the plane at address and impact

Photo 5.52 Right Hand Throw Drill: Right hand square to the plane at midpoint of follow-through

Elbows Back Drill

Stand upright with your elbows pulled back behind your sides and your palms facing forward. Bend forward from the hips so your trunk is in the address position. (Your palms should now be facing slightly downward.)

Now turn your torso as you would on the backswing. While keeping your right elbow up and back, rotate your right wrist and forearm and then bring your left arm across your chest to meet the right hand.

Turn to where your torso faces the ball. Take your left hand away from your right hand and pull your left elbow back, with palm facing forward. Now turn your torso through the impact zone while keeping your left elbow back, and rotate your left wrist and forearm.

Bring your right arm across your chest and let your right hand meet your left in the finish position.

Repeat several times.

Photo 5.53 Elbows Back Drill: At address with both elbows up and back

Photo 5.54 Elbows Back Drill: Turn to the top, reach across with the left arm, and simulate your grip.

Photo 5.55 Elbows Back Drill: Follow-through position with left elbow pulled up and back

Photo 5.56 Elbows Back Drill: Reach across with the right arm and grip the club.

Fault: Arms Disconnecting From Body

Towel Drill

Take a towel and put the two ends together to form a loop. Hold the two ends behind you in your left hand. Put your right hand and arm through the towel loop, then grip a club as at address, with right hand only.

Swing the club to the top of the backswing by pulling the right elbow up and back and pulling the towel tight with the left hand.

While holding the right elbow up and back by keeping the towel tight, practice starting the club back down by dropping your right hand and forearm. As you make this starting-down move, keep pulling on the towel with

Photo 5.57 Towel Drill: Hold towel in left hand and loop around the right elbow.

Photo 5.58 Towel Drill: At the top with the left hand pulling the towel tight and the right elbow up and back

your left hand. This exerts pressure against your right elbow, holding it up and back, along the seam on your right side. As you keep pulling with the left hand against the towel, force the right forearm to drop and swing across the chest to the left.

This drill teaches you the feeling of how the right forearm must work to throw the clubhead out toward the ball, then back around to the left, thus staying on plane through and past impact. Now try this drill hitting a big pitch shot (50 to 75 yards) with about a seven-iron. If you hit behind the ball, you are not swinging your arm around enough to the left. If you are topping the ball, you are not allowing the right forearm to drop enough.

Photo 5.59 Towel Drill: Turn the torso and hit with the right arm while holding the right elbow up and back.

Arms Around Body Drill (Variation 3)
This drill is described on page 106.

Glove Under Arm Drill
This drill is described on page 96.

X Drill (Variation 2)
This drill is described on page 107.

The Two-Plane Address

The setup and posture for the two-plane golfer is actually closer than that of the one-plane golfer to what you might be used to if you have taken lessons or read other instruction books in the past. It is neither a better nor a worse method of setting up to the ball: It is merely a setup that will enhance the strengths of the two-plane swing, which is a more upright and a more arms-dominated action than the one-plane swing.

Model Two-Plane Address Positions

Stance: Narrow Is Better

The stance of the two-plane player should be narrower than that of the one-planer. Not a lot narrower, but enough to be noticeable. For a driver, I'd like to see the insides of your heels be a little narrower than the distance between the outsides of your shoulders—say, about three inches narrower than the desired one-plane stance width. Working your way through the set down to a full pitching wedge, the distance between the heels should be no more than 10 inches, or a good two inches narrower than in the one-plane setup. By narrowing the stance, the lower body will act in a more supportive role to the swinging of the arms, which are the dominant force of the two-plane swing.

The two-plane player, like the one-planer, should strive for squareness in the alignment of all of the body parts. Lines across the toes, knees, hips, and shoulders should all be parallel to a line drawn toward your target. This will hold true for all full shots, except for situations where you need to play a special type of shot where the ball must curve one way or the other. Both the one-plane and two-plane swings have the goal of producing solidly hit, straight shots. Even though the two-plane swing is more hands and arms oriented, this does not mean its goal is any less to strike the ball squarely and straight. Thus, you want to keep your entire body as square to the target as possible, so that no extraordinary manipulations will be needed to get back to square at impact.

A small but important point about the two-plane player's stance is that you should keep your left toe just about perpendicular to the target line, rather than "toeing it out" as the one-plane player does. Keeping the left foot square will allow your hips to turn as fully as possible on the backswing, which increases the swing width the two-plane golfer is looking for.

While the one-planer's weight distribution should slightly favor the left or forward foot, the two-plane golfer's weight should slightly favor the right or rear foot. (The weight should favor the right foot a little more with a driver than with a short iron, where an even weight distribution would be acceptable.) As you may recall, in *The Plane Truth for Golfers* I explained that the two-plane swing, in which the arms move basically upward and downward in front of the body, inherently has a narrower arc than the one-plane swing. Having your weight favoring the rear foot will help you add some desirable width to the two-plane backswing.

120

Posture: Bend Forward Just a Little

The two-plane golfer should bend forward from the hips no more than half as much as the one-plane player. While keeping your back straight by pulling back your shoulder blades as I described in Chapter 2, you should bend forward from the hips by only 10 to 20 degrees from vertical, no more! The key difference here is that, instead of having your shoulders tilted forward much more than your hips, in the two-plane posture your shoulders and hips are set up to turn along the same shallow plane—almost like a merry-go-round would. A good checkpoint for the two-planer is that a line drawn from your shoulders that is perpendicular to your spine at address should point well beyond or outside the 48-inch zone, rather than pointing well within its boundaries.

Photo 6.1 Line perpendicular to the spine should point beyond the zone.

Your arms and hands will automatically be closer in to your body, simply because you are not bent over as much, but the hands should still be approximately underneath your chin.

A common term used for a correct two-plane address position is the "reverse K." To best achieve this position, the two-plane golfer should exhibit a slight leaning (tilt) of the spine and upper body to the right, or away from the target, at address. When you do this, your right shoulder will be slightly lower than your left when viewed from in front. This slight spine tilt is in keeping with the positioning of your weight more on the rear foot. This, too, contributes to a wider swing arc.

Possibly the most noticeable setup difference between one-plane and two-plane players is the positioning of the hands. In keeping with the reverse K position, the two-planer should address the ball with the hands slightly ahead of the clubhead. Instead of the hands being over the left seam of the pants fly, they should be over the left seam of the pants leg. Another way to describe it is that, when viewed from a face-on angle, the club shaft should appear to be an extension of your left arm, with a straight line running all the way from your left shoulder joint down to the clubhead.

In the reverse K setup position, the feeling is of being more under and behind the ball, whereas in the one-plane setup the body appears more symmetric and more directly over the ball.

Grip: Weaker Is Better

I recommend that the two-plane golfer try to develop a grip that is neutral to weak. That is, when you assemble your grip (either the overlap or interlock style), when you look down you should see either the top two knuckles on your left hand (neutral position) or only one knuckle of that hand (weak position).

Photo 6.2 Two-plane reverse K position

You can adjust the position depending on how you normally tend to flight the ball: If you tend to hit the ball straight or with a fade, I'd recommend a neutral position. If you're prone to a hook, the weaker position may suit you.

As mentioned in *The Plane Truth for Golfers*, I prefer two-plane golfers to go with a slightly weaker grip position than a one-plane golfer would, because the neutral-to-weak grip encourages a clubface that tends to be a bit more open, rather than closed, throughout its movement along the swing arc. Furthermore, a more open clubface tends to encourage a little more width in the swing arc, which the two-plane golfer can always benefit from.

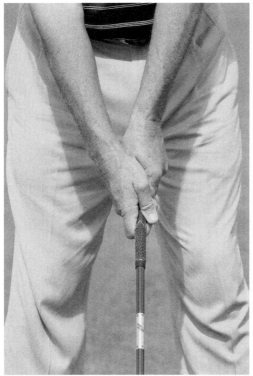

Photo 6.3 Neutral grip

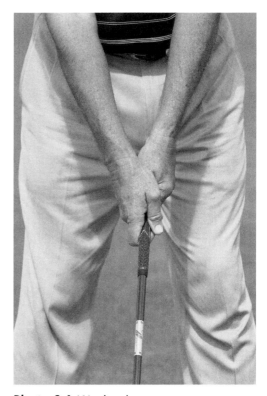

Photo 6.4 Weak grip

Ball Position: Get Closer

The ball position in relation to your feet, as viewed from in front, is the same as that for the one-plane player: Opposite the left heel to left instep with a driver, gradually working back to the center of the stance for a full pitching wedge. (Of course, the ball position can be moved outside this range when the lie and/or wind conditions call for a special type of ball flight.) What is different is that the two-planer will stand a relatively shorter distance from the ball. This is simply a result of the fact that you have bent your spine forward much less than the one-plane player would. Since your head is less bent over, and your hands are still comfortably placed underneath a line drawn down from your chin, it stands to reason that you will be noticeably closer in to the ball for all normal full shots.

LESSON: Common Two-Plane Setup Problems and Corrections

There are several common faults in the setup of players trying to develop a two-plane swing that to a great degree sabotage the effort before they have drawn the club back. These errors are as follows:

1. The player's shoulders are open in relation to the target line, while the hips tend to be closed to the target.
2. The player has too much weight on the left (forward) foot.
3. While the amount of forward bend in the spine is usually acceptable, the player's shoulders are slumped forward.
4. When viewed from a face-on angle, the spine is tilted slightly to the left (toward the target). The shoulders are level instead of the left shoulder being higher than the right.

Photo 6.5 Two-plane address fault with open shoulders, poor posture, and hands too high

Photo 6.6 Two-plane address fault with too much weight on the left leg and spine tilt to the left

5. When viewed from down-target, the hands are too high and are well in front of a line drawn down from the chin.

Again, in correcting these setup problems, you may need to overcorrect these errors, as described in Chapter 2. Check that you are overcorrecting either by using a mirror or by having a friend watch you take your two-plane address.

1. Open shoulders are one of the biggest address problems for the two-plane golfer. This goes hand-in-hand with having too much weight on the front foot. It is easy to have open shoulders at address simply because in reaching your right hand below your left on the grip, your right shoulder is pulled forward somewhat. In addition, when you have your hands leading the clubhead (two-plane players, as a rule, seem to place them correctly for their method), this also serves to push the left shoulder back or away from the target line somewhat. So, considering all these factors, you may have to consciously work on getting your shoulders square to your target line. This might well mean that you have to overcorrect for a while, so that your shoulders are actually closed to the target line. Have a friend hold a club across the front of your shoulders and be sure it is pointing parallel to your target line or a little to the right of it.

Photo 6.7 Two-plane square shoulder correction

At the same time, more amateurs that I see have their hips closed than open. Get in the habit of feeling that you're setting up with your hips a little open. This may feel strange at first, but remember that your ultimate goal is to set up with all of your body parts lined up squarely to the target.

2. Move your weight back so that at least 50 percent, preferably a little more, is on your right or rear foot.

3. While your spine angle is probably fine (bent forward just 10 to 20 degrees), you want your back to be straight, not curved with your shoulders slumped forward. Pull

Photo 6.8 Two-plane spine tilt correction

126

your shoulder blades back while standing upright (which makes it nearly impossible to slump the shoulders forward), then bend forward from the hips between 10 and 20 degrees, but no more.

4. Move the tilt of your spine from slightly toward the target to slightly away from it. As you do this, your right shoulder should drop to a position that's noticeably lower than your left shoulder.

This will also help you to square up the shoulders, particularly if you tend to have your shoulders open too much at address. The two-plane player will also find it helpful to bend the right knee just a trifle more than the left, which will also get the right side a bit lower.

5. Relax your hands and arms so they drop inward, underneath your chin, but there are still a few inches of clearance between your hands and the front of your body.

Fact Versus Feel

If you were previously accustomed to the more symmetric setup of the one-plane golfer (wittingly or unwittingly) and are now attempting to develop the two-plane setup, the two-plane setup I have described will feel quite different. You will probably **feel** like your head is a foot behind the ball, even though in **fact** you've only moved the head back two or three inches. Your right shoulder may **feel** as though it is dragging on the ground. In addition, you may **feel** as if so much weight is on your right foot that you're close to losing your balance during the backswing. But remember, the changes, in **fact**, are not as severe as you may think, even if you are overcorrecting on all of them at the start. Keep monitoring your address position in the mirror or with a friend; even though it may seem tiresome, it will make the execution of the two-plane swing (to be described in the following chapters), much easier to accomplish successfully.

The Two-Plane Backswing

In this chapter, I describe the ideal movements of the two-plane backswing, breaking down the action into two parts: body movements and positions and arm and club movements and positions. In addition, I explain common problems that golfers experience when trying to execute the two-plane backswing. Along with these explanations of common errors, I describe the most common ball flight patterns that result from each given error. In the Fact Versus Feel segment at the end of each lesson, I review the realities and sensations you will experience as you implement these new swing moves into your two-plane backswing. Finally, I complete my instructional message by listing drills that will help you to understand and accomplish the two-plane swing moves.

Part One: Model Two-Plane Backswing Body Movements

There is one element of the two-plane backswing that is identical to that of the one-plane swing. It is that you turn your shoulders as fully as you can. The two-plane backswing differs in that you also turn your hips as fully as you can. The turn of your upper body will, however, be significantly different from the one-planer's upper body turn, in a couple of ways. The most significant difference is that your shoulder turn will be much flatter, or closer to that of a merry-go-round, than that of the one-plane golfer. The reason for this is that in the two-plane address, you tilt your spine forward at address much less than

Photo 7.1 Two-plane correct shoulder turn beyond the zone

the one-planer does—only 10 to 20 degrees of forward spine bend, as opposed to 35 to 45 degrees of forward bend for the one-planer. Since you should turn your shoulders perpendicular to your spine angle, it is only natural and correct for the plane of your shoulder turn to be just 10 to 20 degrees downward from horizontal. To put it another way, when you turn your shoulders 90 degrees from the address position, a line across your shoulders should point well outside the zone, that 48-inch area that extends along the ground from the ball outward.

It's a good idea to ask a friend to help you check this. If a line across your shoulders at the top of the backswing points anywhere inside the zone, it means one of two errors is occurring: either your spine angle is bent forward too much at address, or you are tilting your left shoulder down and your right shoulder up rather than making a pure turn around your spine.

Meanwhile, unlike the one-plane golfer, you are also going to turn your hips freely and fully on the backswing. The two-plane address position encourages you to do this, because your shoulders and hips are set on about the same angle of forward bend (10 to 20 degrees). This means that your shoulders and your hips should turn on nearly identical planes during the backswing, allowing your hips to turn almost as far as your shoulders do on the backswing. Don't try to restrict your hip turn in any way. (I'd like to add here that as a two-plane player you may find that you can make a larger shoulder turn than you could if you were set up in the one-plane swinger's address position. This is because, with your shoulders and hips turning on the same plane, there will be much less tension between the upper and lower halves of the body. The free turn of your hips thus makes it easier for the shoulders to turn a little farther than they would if the shoulders and hips were turning on significantly different plane angles.)

Be that as it may, you should allow your hips to turn as much as they want, as long as the hips stay centered over your feet. As you swing back, you should feel your weight moving predominantly onto your right or rear foot and that you are getting your upper body more behind the ball. In fact, in the two-plane backswing, it is allowable for your spine and head to tilt slightly to the right, or away from your target, as the shoulders turn.

As I explained in *The Plane Truth for Golfers*, a little bit of spine tilt in this direction is acceptable for the two-planer, because the two-plane swing arc is inherently narrower than the one-plane swing arc. Furthermore, a slight spine tilt will add a little width to your backswing. It is okay if your head moves back several inches from its original position on a full driver shot. For the shorter irons, I'd rather see your spine and head stay pretty much centered over the ball.

Photo 7.2 Two-plane correct top of backswing maintaining spine tilt behind the ball

With regard to the forward bend of the spine, you may recall that I warned one-plane golfers against letting the spine angle rise at any point during the swing. The two-planer, on the other hand, should not *lower* his or her spine angle either on the backswing or the downswing, as this will serve to reduce the already-narrow swing arc even more. Raising the spine angle a bit is not usually a problem for the two-planer: Remember, a two-plane golfer will be swinging the arms up while the body is turning around, so it is a little more likely that the spine angle may also rise slightly during the backswing. Just don't consciously try to raise the spine angle. It's a good idea to have a friend monitor your spine angle as you make your backswing, making sure that your head does not move up more than two inches.

As you reach the top of the two-plane backswing, both your hips and your shoulders will have turned well away from the ball. Your weight should be primarily on your right or rear foot. The two-planer will also usually reach the top with his or her left heel turned well inward, to the right, or with the left heel completely off the ground. This position of the left heel is quite different than that of the one-plane swinger. It occurs in response to the fact that you have turned your hips much farther around from the address position, and your left heel has risen in response to your full hip turn. This is fine; just don't make any conscious effort to lift the heel on the backswing.

In summary, then, at the top of the two-plane backswing you should feel as if you are more turned behind the ball with the upper body, as opposed to directly over it.

132

LESSON: Curing a Reverse Pivot Problem

A two-plane golfer develops a reverse pivot at the top primarily because of one or more of three faults: The player has not turned the shoulders fully enough; the player has slid the hips laterally to the right, rather than turning them; or the player has rotated the hips either too far or too fast to coordinate the hip turn with the shoulder turn.

I would say that either sliding the hips or rotating them too fast is the most common fault. Whichever of the three faults or combination of faults is happening, this player winds up with too much weight on the left or forward foot at the top; and while the player's spine angle is usually acceptable (the angle is similar

Photo 7.3 Two-plane reverse pivot fault with underrotated shoulders

Photo 7.4 Two-plane reverse pivot fault with lateral hip slide

Photo 7.5 Two-plane reverse pivot fault with incorrect hip pivot

to that at address, when viewed from down-target), this player's spine will probably tilt somewhat to the left, or toward the target, when viewed from a face-on angle. Obviously, any tilting toward the target is undesirable for the two-plane golfer, as it shrinks the width of this player's swing arc even more.

The two-plane player who reverse pivots will struggle with the same pattern of erratic and poorly struck shots that the one-plane golfer will: namely, fat, popped-up shots; steep tops (clubface meets top of ball on the way down); shots pulled straight left; and very weak left-to-right slices. If anything, the two-plane golfer with a reverse pivot will hit even worse shots than a one-plane golfer with the same fault, because when a two-plane golfer reverse pivots, his or her downswing will be extremely steep and narrow. With the club moving down this steeply, there will be very little energy left to propel the ball forward.

To solve this seriously faulty swing pattern, your first thought should be to turn your chest and shoulders away from the ball as fully as you can. A good thought to help you accomplish this is, "Turn your back to the target."

Once your shoulders have started rotating on a shallow angle, let your hips go along with your shoulder turn. Given your address position, the hips can and will turn nearly as much as your shoulders, as long as you don't make any conscious effort to restrict them. As you complete this full hip turn, your left heel will likely be pulled slightly off the ground. Just remember that your backswing turn should flow in this sequence: shoulders/torso, then hips, then left heel.

As you make your backswing turn, make certain you can feel your weight distribution flowing onto your right or rear foot. As you swing back, keep your spine angle up (if anything, raising it a touch rather than lowering it). As you reach the top of the backswing, have a friend observe you from a face-on view to make sure that your spine has tilted to the right or away from the ball, if anything. A two-plane player's spine should never tilt toward the target.

There are a couple of drills that I think will help if you are a two-plane player who reverse pivots. These are the Club Across Shoulders Drill (Variation 4) and the Wallet Pocket Left Drill. Descriptions of all drills for the two-plane player appear in Chapter 9.

Fact Versus Feel

Almost everyone who has ever played the game of golf has heard the stern admonition, "Keep your head still!" This is the same thing as telling a golfer not to move his or her upper body either up, down, toward, or away from the target during the swing (although the emphasis on keeping your head still is directed more, I believe, toward whether it moves laterally than up or down). While this basically holds true for the one-plane player, it is a **fact** that the two-plane golfer will benefit from a moderate lateral movement to the right, or away from the target, on the backswing. Allowing this will add width to this player's swing arc.

Of course, you must make sure not to move laterally to such a degree that you get your weight to the outside of your right or rear foot so that you lose balance. Keep checking your backswing in a mirror. If you see a slight lateral movement of the head away from the target, that should be fine.

Meanwhile, you will have a number of different sensations as you execute the backswing. It will **feel** as though your shoulders are turning level to the ground; or to put it another way, your left shoulder will feel high and your right shoulder low. This is fine, as long as you are turning your shoulders around your spine angle rather than tilting them. Similarly, your left hip will **feel** as if it's much higher than normal (although it will be higher, the difference in **fact** is very slight). The left hip should also **feel** as if it is much farther to the left; that is, the left hip should not feel as if it has slid laterally to the right, the way the reverse-pivot player's hips typically do.

Photo 7.6 Two-plane with correct slight shift to the right in backswing

Last, if you are used to keeping your head and spine directly over the ball at the top of the backswing, it may **feel** as though your head is about four feet behind the ball, that your backswing is extremely wide, and that you will never be able to get back to the ball by the point of impact. The **fact** is that, yes, your head and upper body are farther behind the ball, but it is a difference of perhaps three to four inches with a driver, and less (if any) with the shorter clubs. You are still in balance, and you are fully capable of the slight lateral shift toward the target on the downswing that will allow you to make solid contact.

LESSON: Curing an Insufficient Backswing Turn Fault

An insufficient turning action is the problem the two-plane golfer exhibits most frequently. The player simply does not turn and get far enough behind the ball on the backswing to create the speed and the width of swing arc needed to hit powerful shots.

Among the amateurs who struggle to make a good turn, it seems to me that the problem lies more in their lack of hip turn than in their upper body turn. True, both the upper and lower bodies do not turn far enough. But more often, it's the player's failure to allow the hips to turn freely that prevents the shoulders from turning as far as they should.

It seems to me that a lot of amateurs who are two-plane swingers (whether they know it or not) have developed this problem because of a swing theory that has been popular for a number of years. This theory is known as the X Factor. Basically, the X Factor means that the golfer should

Photo 7.7 Two-plane fault of insufficient backswing turn

turn the shoulders as far as he or she can, while consciously restricting the turn of the hips. As we have seen, this concept is okay if you're a one-plane swinger. (Even for the one-planer, though, I would say the concept of the X Factor is not perfect. That's because even the one-planer should not consciously resist turning the hips. It's the difference in the planes that the shoulders and the hips turn on that serves to restrict the hip turn on the backswing.) However, I believe that trying to implement the X Factor by restricting the hip turn is extremely harmful for the two-plane swinger.

Although the specific label "two-plane swing" was not in vogue during Jack Nicklaus's prime years, Nicklaus was a classic two-plane golfer. I am thankful that Nicklaus recognized the need, in his type of swing at least, to turn the hips fully and freely on the backswing and to allow the left heel to rise to facilitate that big hip turn, and stressed this frequently in his own instruction. So thank you, Jack, for giving the two-plane golfer that ideal advice regarding the backswing turn.

The two-plane golfer with insufficient turn usually does not have severe problems with weight distribution and spine angle. He or she should make sure the majority of the weight shifts onto the right or rear foot at the top of the backswing, perhaps allowing a little more of this weight shift than he or she does currently. This golfer's spine angle usually stays pretty constant on the backswing—the more complete turn may tend to raise it slightly, and this is also okay. The player's spine usually tilts slightly to the right, and it will do so a little more when the entire body-turn increases.

The ball flight of the two-plane swinger who does not turn enough is probably the least predictable of all the faulty ball flights we have discussed so far. This is because (and you'll understand this more fully after we discuss the role of the arms and the club for the two-planer) this player's swing path is on too much of what I call a "straight-line" path. That is, due to insufficient body rotation, the club does not swing far enough inside the target line on the backswing, and it does not swing far enough or quickly enough back to the inside after impact.

"Wait a minute," I can hear you saying right now. "What's wrong with swinging the club more along the target line throughout the swing? Wouldn't that help to guarantee that I'll hit the ball straighter?" Well, that's a very astute question, because on the surface, it would seem that a swing that moves the club on a path close to the target line might help you hit the ball straighter. But it won't, and here's why.

When you have a swing that stays too close to the target line, it means you have a swing that has very little body turn and a lot of lifting of the club with the arms. However, you must still cock the club to get it to the top of the backswing, which we have seen can often put the club shaft in a laid-off position relative to the target.

Then you pull the club down with very little body turn, just as you took it back. At some point in this type of downswing, you are going to have to rotate the clubface from open to square to closed with your hands and arms. Moreover, this rotation usually happens so quickly and so close to impact that the timing must be absolutely perfect, or else the clubface can come into the ball either wide open or dead closed. So this player has the worst of all worlds, you might say. He or she can hit a big, diving duck hook on one swing and then a weak, popped-up slice on the next.

Of course, this golfer is also prone to both fat and thin shots, because this type of swing has a very small "bottom"—in other words, there is very little space in which the clubhead is moving close to or at ground level. Thus this player will hit behind the ball a lot, or he or she will top the ball on the upswing.

If you have an insufficient body turn, you must actively turn your shoulders as well as your hips. Make

Photo 7.8 Two-plane fault of insufficient turn and club shaft laid off

sure that you initiate your backswing with the turning of your shoulders. This will be followed by the hip turn, and finally the lifting of the left heel. If you do these three things, the majority of your weight will shift onto your right or rear foot as it should. If your spine angle should rise a little bit as you near the top of the backswing, that's okay. Likewise, if you make the free turn of the entire body as described, chances are your spine will tilt and your head will move a little to the right, which again is acceptable as it will add width to your swing arc.

It's a good idea to practice your entire backswing in front of a mirror; or better yet, have a friend observe your backswing from a position facing you. Make sure that he or she is aware of and looking for each of the checkpoints we have discussed.

The key **fact** for the two-plane golfer is that he or she must turn both the torso and the hips as fully as possible on the backswing. The shoulder turn will lead the body turn, or to put it another way, the hips will start their turn in response to the turn of the shoulders. Also, as the torso and hips turn, the spine should tilt slightly right, or else a reverse pivot becomes likely. Given those two stipulations, you cannot turn your hips too far in the two-plane swing.

When you make the ideal two-plane backswing, it will **feel** as though your shoulders and your hips have turned way too far in a clockwise direction. You will think that the backswing plane you've created is extremely wide, and far to the inside. This is a normal sensation. At the top of the backswing, it will **feel** as though you will end up hitting the ball with the club traveling too much from inside-out, so that you will either hit a straight push to the right or a big, sweeping hook. This, too, is a positive sensation if you had previously been lifting the club rather than turning the body. Finally (and this is especially true with the driver), you might actually turn to the point where you lose sight of the ball for an instant as you reach the top of the swing. Again, as long as your weight is over the center of your right foot, meaning you have not swayed off balance, this is okay also in the two-plane backswing. Remember that you will be coupling these turning and lateral movements of the body with a number of vertical actions by your arms and the club. When you put these components together in the finished swing, you will see that they end up counterbalancing one another very nicely. So let's move on now to see just how your arms and the club should move in the effective two-plane swing.

Part Two: Two-Plane Backswing Arms and Club Movements and Positions

The movement of your arms in the two-plane backswing is vastly different from that of the one-plane swinger. In the one-plane backswing and downswing, you are swinging your arms around the torso. In the two-plane swing, you will essentially be keeping your arms in front of your torso. While your shoulders

Photo 7.9 Two-plane arms swing up in front of the body

Photo 7.10 Two-plane backswing body turn

Photo 7.11 Two-plane correct backswing with blend of upward arm swing and body turn

and hips turn, you will swing your arms straight up during the backswing and then back down on the downswing.

A good overall image of the two-plane swing is to think of making a turn with your body while you execute a karate chop movement with your arms. The two-plane swing is in essence the combination of a nearly horizontal turn of the body with a nearly vertical driving of the arms.

In the ideal two-plane backswing, the arm swing and the shoulder turn will be a smooth, simultaneous movement. Your left forearm (and with it the club) should move slightly inside the target line as a response to the initial shoulder turn. You need not make a conscious move to get the hands or the club inside the target line.

As your shoulders continue to turn, along with your hips, on a shallow or flat plane, you should begin to fold your right elbow. This right elbow fold allows the left arm and the right forearm to begin to move up in front of the right half of your chest (for right-handed golfers). This upward move will lift the clubhead with it, so that the plane that is beginning to be described by the clubhead is steeper (more like a Ferris wheel) than that of the one-plane swinger.

When you reach a point halfway into the backswing, with the club shaft parallel to the ground and parallel to the target line, the club shaft should be a little farther out away

Photo 7.12 Two-plane midpoint backswing with club shaft vertically over tips of shoes

from your body than for the one-plane golfer. That is to say, it should be over a line that drops down to the front edge of your shoes, as opposed to being over your insteps.

This is because in the two-plane swing, there is no inward pulling with your right arm on the backswing to bring the club in tighter to you, just a turn of the body along with the beginning of the upward lifting of the arms. Another difference at this point in the backswing is that the toe of your club should be pointing straight up, not angled as the one-plane player's should be when viewed from behind. As you recall from earlier discussion of the one-plane backswing, when the toe is pointing straight up, it is actually somewhat open in relation to the plane of the one-plane swing. The two-plane swing is more upright, and the arms move much more up and down, with very little rotation. Therefore the club should be more toe up at this point, much as if you just raised your arms waist high in front of you and turned your body, you would find the club would be toe up.

As you continue the backswing, keep swinging your right forearm and your left arm up in front of the right side of your chest, as your chest and hips continue their turn. In the second half of the backswing, the movement of your arms is purely a lifting motion. It is the continued turning of your torso that will set the club into position behind you at the top of the backswing. If you have made the lifting motion with your arms correctly, at the top of the backswing your hands and the club shaft will be noticeably higher than for the one-plane player. If your club shaft reaches a position parallel to the ground at the top, an observer standing in front of you would be able to see the entire club shaft, which is slightly higher than your head. By comparison, the one-plane player's club shaft will be lower than the head at the top.

Great examples of players with these "high hands" at the top of the two-plane backswing are Tom Watson and Davis Love (although Love's hands were even higher in the past than they are today) and, among today's younger tour players, David Toms.

At the top of the backswing, it frequently occurs that the two-plane golfer's club shaft will point to the right of his or her target. This is commonly referred to as "crossing the line" at the top. To a large degree your club's position at the top will depend on how far you turn your torso and hips on the backswing. Power hitter John Daly has a backswing that not only is very long but also crosses the line very noticeably. In general, for the two-plane golfer, the club shaft should point either parallel to the target line or be crossing the line slightly at the top.

As to the position of the clubface itself, while I prefer that the one-plane swinger have a clubface that is a little closed throughout the swing,

Photo 7.13 Two-plane top of backswing with club shaft above head

I'd rather see the two-planer have a clubface that is square to slightly open at the top of the backswing. If you recall from the detailed discussion in Chapter 3 about the position of the club at the top of the backswing, essentially, the golfer must cock the club behind him or her in order to complete the backswing, so that technically every golfer's clubface is to some degree open to the plane at the top of the backswing. However, in terms of the top-of-backswing position of the club, you remember that the conventional interpretation of squareness was that the club's toe would be pointing halfway between pointing downward (completely open) and pointing parallel to the ground (completely closed). Within this definition, whereas I recommend that the one-plane swinger's clubface be slightly on the closed side, for the two-planer, the clubface should be if anything a shade open (toe pointing more downward than parallel to the ground). This is in keeping with the fact that the clubface was already in an open position halfway back, and is also useful in that any movements that open the clubface will add width to the swing, which always helps the two-plane swinger.

Let's now discuss the most common errors I see in the movements of the arms and the club in the two-plane backswing.

LESSON: Correcting Arms Outside/Narrow Plane Problems

Here is the case of the golfer who does a good job of hoisting the club upward, but does not have enough inward-and-around turning of the body. This can be a problem either of lack of movement, meaning the turn of the body is insufficient; or it can be a matter of poor timing, in which the arms are going up faster than the body is making its turn. Usually when this player gets the club halfway back (when the club shaft is parallel to the ground), the shaft will not point directly back from the target (when viewed from behind), but rather point to outside the target line. Also, the club shaft will appear to be well in front of the shoes rather than directly over the toe line.

This club shaft position indicates that the lifting of the arms is happening at a faster rate than the turning of the body. When the player has more or faster lifting than turning, he or she will usually manage to get the clubface relatively open at the top; however, because of the relative lack of body turn the club shaft will often be laid off at the top (pointing left of the target line).

Photo 7.14 Two-plane fault of club shaft too far away from body and outside the target line

Photo 7.15 Two-plane fault of club shaft laid off at top of backswing

A good example of a successful player with this type of backswing is Colin Montgomerie. Montgomerie is able to reroute the club at the start of the downswing in such a way that his downswing is less steep and less from outside-in, but he still has a slightly outside-in path through impact, hence he almost always hits his shots with a left-to-right fade.

Montgomerie aside, most golfers with this type of two-plane backswing will end up bringing the club into the ball on a steep, outside-in swing path. By now you can probably guess what that means in terms of the flight of the ball: lots of big slices, pulls to the left, fat, popped-up shots, and steep tops with the clubhead descending on top of the ball. This player also usually takes very deep divots. Alternatively, this player may try to reroute the club to the inside at the start of the downswing, but this requires near-perfect timing, tempo, and balance and rarely results in consistent shot-making.

To solve the problem, you must work on the timing of your movements of the arms and the body. You need to swing your arms up a little bit slower and turn your body, particularly the hips, a little sooner. By turning your body a little sooner, your arms will automatically come more inward rather than straight up. When you do this, you should begin to see the club shaft pointing directly away from the target when the club is parallel to the ground halfway back. The shaft should then be positioned closer in to your body, over the insteps instead of outside the toes. Also at this point in the backswing, the toe of the club should be pointing straight up. Practice taking the club back to this position in slow motion, in front of a mirror. You'll see that you have to turn your shoulder and hips in a circular fashion at about the same rate that you start to fold your right elbow and lift the club up.

From here, continue to turn the entire body as you lift your arms and the club up to the top. In a full backswing where the club shaft reaches a position parallel to the ground, it should be crossing the line so that it points to the right of the target. This is a slightly exaggerated position, but is certainly a correct option for a two-planer and is the opposite position at the top from the golfer's usual laid-off position.

A good drill if you are trying to develop the necessary timing of the two turns is the Turn and Face Club Drill, which is described in Chapter 9.

Fact Versus Feel

It is a **fact** that if you've developed a too-narrow arc in the two-plane swing, you'll need to practice the blending of the upward motion of the arms with the turning of the body by trial and error. You may in fact overcompensate for a while, that is, turn your body more or faster than you lift your arms, so that you may hit some shots that indicate the opposite problems from what is normal for you. Keep adjusting the two movements. It's like constantly adjusting the steering wheel of a ship that is bouncing around on heavy seas. Gradually you will start timing the motions so they're closer and closer to an ideal mix.

Photo 7.16 Two-plane **feel** of arms and club shaft inside

Photo 7.17 Two-plane **feel** of club shaft across the line at top of backswing

Until you have accomplished this, however, you will **feel** as if your arms and the club are coming back far more to the inside than they should (which is to say, your arms feel like they're going more inward than upward).

Your body will **feel** as if it is turning much sooner, particularly your hips. Indeed, you will feel like you've turned your body 90 degrees from the address position by the time your club has reached halfway back. All these sensations are normal if you've been lifting the club with a narrow arc for any length of time. As you move the club and turn your body to the finish of the backswing, the club will **feel** as though it is across the line. If in fact it is slightly across the line, that's okay.

Keep working on your timing of the arm and body movements, particularly with the Turn and Face Club Drill, while checking your progress in a mirror, and you'll soon get the club on a more desirable track.

LESSON: The Art of Fixing
an Arms Too Inside/Around Body Fault

Here is a two-plane golfer with the opposite problem: He or she is turning the body rapidly away from the ball, but is not lifting the arms and the club concurrently. The golfer is either turning his or her body (particularly the hips) too early or too quickly; or the player's arms are moving upward too slowly; or they are not moving upward at all. (See photo 7.16 in Lesson: Correcting Arms Outside/Narrow Plane Problems.)

At the halfway point in the backswing (club shaft parallel to ground at about hip height), this golfer's club will not point straight back but will be angled well inward, or to the left when viewed from down-target. If and when the player does finally lift the club with his or her arms, the club shaft will almost always cross the line or point right of the target. (See photo 7.17 in Lesson: Correcting Arms Outside/Narrow Plane Problems.) Impact will likely occur with the club moving on a shallow, inside-out plane. The resulting ball flight will include lots of fat or thin shots, pushed shots, toe hooks, and shallow tops (top of ball hit on the upswing). Occasionally golfers with this backswing problem will overcompensate from their "too far inside" position in the backswing and will violently over-turn their body in relation to their arm swing during the downswing and as a result will be very steep and out-to-in. In either downswing case, the root problem is a backswing that is too far to the inside, and from here it is too difficult to recover correctly in a consistent manner.

147

If you're struggling with this problem, you need to work hard on timing your body turn with the lifting of the arms, but you need to adjust in the opposite way to the previous lesson. You must move your arms up in front of the right side of the chest a little sooner in the backswing. Meanwhile, you need to begin your body turn a little more slowly than you have been. Particularly, you should focus on making your hip turn a little more slowly in order to get the arms moving upward concurrently. If you are synchronizing these moves correctly, with the club halfway back on the backswing your club shaft should be parallel to the target line and above a line directly over your toes. The club's toe should be pointing straight up, or open in relation to your swing path. Practice lifting your arms and turning your body in slow motion in front of a mirror until you can get the club into the position described.

A great drill if you are swinging your arms too much to the inside is the Stand Near a Wall Drill, which is described in Chapter 9.

Fact Versus Feel

If you are a two-planer struggling with the arms and club coming too much inside, it's a **fact** that you must adjust the timing of your movements along the contrasting planes of the two-plane swing. When you start your arms swinging up earlier, it will **feel** as if you are taking the club very much to the outside. (See photo 7.14 in Lesson: Correcting Arms Outside/Narrow Plane Problems.) The backswing will also feel very steep and narrow compared to what you are used to. At the same time, your body turn, particularly with the hips, will **feel** very slow or late in relation to your arm lift. As with the two-plane golfer whose swing arc is too narrow, you will need to keep adjusting until you can see in a mirror (from a down-target angle) that the two movements are blended well together. If they are, the club will move up along a consistent plane all the way to the top of the backswing, with no late adjustments by either the arms or the body necessary. At the top of the backswing, the club shaft will **feel** pointed to the left or laid off (see photo 7.15 in Lesson: Correcting Arms Outside/Narrow Plane Problems), when in actual **fact** you want it to be pointed right at your target.

8

The Two-Plane Downswing

In this chapter, I discuss what it takes to successfully blend the ingredients of the two-plane downswing. After discussing the ideal movements of the body and of the arms and club, I will give you lessons on how to correct the most common faults most amateurs make, again including Fact Versus Feel segments to better relay my instruction and help you improve more quickly.

Part One: Two-Plane Downswing Body Movements

The first move from the top by the two-plane swinger must be a lateral shift of the left hip to the left (toward the target). When you complete the move, the hip should be slightly closer to the target than the outside of your left foot.

A fraction of a second later, you should begin turning your hips in a counterclockwise direction (for right-handers) and keep turning them all the way through impact and follow-through. The shoulders will follow the turning lead of the hips. In the full driver downswing, if you have made a correct, fully turned backswing, you should try to turn your hips and shoulders a full 180 degrees, if not more, from the top of the backswing through the completion of the follow-through. Assuming you have moderate flexibility in your midsection, at the finish your hips should be facing the target and your shoulders should have turned slightly beyond the point where they are directly facing the target, and they should be fairly level with the ground.

Throughout the downswing, the amount of weight on your left foot should be constantly increasing until, at the finish, you are up on your right toe, with nearly 100 percent of your weight on the left foot.

A couple of comments about your spine angle and tilt. As you swing down toward and through impact, the two-plane golfer's spine angle should stay the same or even rise slightly. Meanwhile, your spine (when viewed from face-on) should remain tilted slightly to the right, or away from the target, through impact. This is because your head should remain steady in its position behind the ball until after the ball is struck.

This slight spine tilt and head position to the right, while the weight has shifted onto the left foot, leads the golfer to a finish that is a slight version of the classic reverse C position, with the hips more forward and the head and shoulders back, as opposed to the finish of the one-plane golfer, whose upper body will be stacked more directly over the left leg. Do not overdo this "stay

Photo 8.1 Two-plane start of downswing with lateral hip move

Photo 8.2 Two-plane finish with weight fully on left leg

Photo 8.3 Two-plane correct finish with head still slightly behind the ball

behind the ball" spine tilt, however—it will develop into too much of the reverse C position and will cause back problems.

The player developing a two-plane downswing needs to beware of a couple of specific problems, so let me discuss them in lesson form.

LESSON: Correcting a Shoulders-Turning-Early Problem

Some two-planers have difficulty with the timing of their downswing because, instead of starting with a lateral thrust of the left hip, they immediately turn their shoulders fast and hard as the first move in the downswing. The shoulders also get ahead of the downward driving of the arms. Thus this player exhibits a classic over-the-top, outside-in downswing path.

The reason this player comes over the top (while the one-plane swinger does not) is that, as you recall, the two-plane golfer sets up his or her shoulders on a plane that's much closer to horizontal than the one-plane golfer's. Thus, if the shoulders start down first, moving along the plane set up at address, the golfer will throw the clubhead well outside the correct plane, just as a line across the two-plane golfer's shoulders point well outside or beyond the zone at the top of the backswing.

Since the hips have not initiated the backswing with a lateral slide to the left, this golfer's weight is usually a little too much on the right or rear foot during the down-swing. Usually, the forward bend of the spine (the spine angle) is not a significant problem. However, because of the immediate over-the-top move of the shoulders, the spine tilt

Photo 8.4 Two-plane fault of early downswing shoulder turn

when viewed from in front is either straight up or tilted left, with the head moving toward the target.

As a result of the overly dominant shoulder movement, this golfer cannot help but bring the club down on a steep, outside-in path. He or she will hit fat, popped shots, steep topped shots (contacting the top of the ball with the clubhead descending), and either straight pulls or big slices, depending on whether the clubface was flipped to closed at impact (pull) or left open in relation to that outside-in path (big slice).

If this sounds like your pattern, you can correct most of your downswing problems by initiating the downswing with a lateral slide of the hips directly at the target. It can be exaggerated into a pronounced bump hip slide and still be okay for this golfer.

When you slide the hips laterally, notice how your entire right side, from the waist up to the shoulder, will drop straight down; and your arms, hands, and the club will make a pronounced downward drop along with it. You must feel your hip slide and your arm drop before you start turning your hips or shoulders horizontally. Strive to keep your back facing the target for that extra instant

Photo 8.5 Two-plane early shoulder turn fault with spine tilt to the left

Photo 8.6 Two-plane correction with exaggerated lateral hip move

so that you feel your arms dropping before you let your shoulders begin to unwind.

As you swing down, you should keep your spine fairly erect, never bending forward more than the 10 to 20 degrees it was bent forward at address. Also, make sure your head stays back, behind the ball, all the way through impact. When you keep your head back in this manner, your spine will be tilted slightly to the right when viewed from a face-on angle. Finally, as you turn your body through and beyond impact, you should feel that almost all of your weight below your waist is on your left or forward foot.

Practice with the Hip Slide/Arm Drop Drill in Chapter 9 will help you get the two-plane downswing off to a good start.

Fact Versus Feel

When you make the lateral slide with your hips, it's a **fact** that the outside of your hip should reach a point slightly outside (or closer to the target than) the outside of the left foot.

Although the left hip will **feel** as if it's much higher than your right or rear hip, the **fact** is that it is actually only slightly higher as you move from the start of the downswing through impact. Likewise, it will **feel** as though your spine is tilted way to the right; in **fact** it should only be slightly tilted in that direction.

153

Although you will be turning your shoulders more or less around your spine through the downswing, it will **feel** as if your shoulders are tilting rather than turning. In **fact**, they are turning, but they are somewhat tilted as they turn because in the downswing, as in the two-plane setup and backswing, the right or rear shoulder is held lower than the left (remember the reverse K address position of the two-plane golfer). However, the actual movement of the shoulders is indeed a turn on a nearly horizontal plane around your spine.

When you delay the uncoiling of your shoulders as advised, it will **feel** as though your back is still facing the target almost until impact. In reality, your shoulders will start unwinding just a fraction of a second after you slide your left hip and drop your arms.

Last, when you begin to make the correct two-plane body moves as described, it will **feel** as though at impact, you're swinging up on the ball and also swinging very much out to the right of your target. In some cases, if you make an overcorrection on some or all of the various body movements we've discussed, it may indeed become a **fact** that you're swinging the club from the inside-out, so that you start hooking the ball.

This is a good sign, and it should be relatively easy for you to readjust the movement. You can do this by simply beginning the shoulder turn just a fraction earlier; another effective way to adjust is to make your hip slide/arm drop move just a little less forcefully.

Photo 8.7 Two-plane inside-out

LESSON: Fixing Lateral Slide/Too Much Tilt Faults

This is the golfer who has plenty of lateral motion in his or her downswing; however, the second element of the two-plane downswing, the turning of the hips and shoulders, is lacking.

This golfer usually does a good job of starting the downswing by driving the left or lead hip laterally at the target. When this happens, the left hip leads, most of the weight shifts onto the left foot, and the upper body is somewhat behind, with the spine tilted to the right when viewed from face-on in front. All this is fine, up to a point. However, this golfer has not immediately followed the lateral thrust with a full turning of the body (hips and shoulders). Because there has been very little rotation, the upper body gets left way behind the hips, with the head sliding away from the target.

A golfer who slides laterally but does not turn the body through and beyond impact usually ends up with a downswing that is on too much of a straight-line path through the ball—very similar to the downswing of the one-plane golfer who does not turn the shoulders actively enough. Since the upper body, and with it the arms and the club, are left behind the lower body, what happens most often is that the player's downswing "bottoms out" behind the ball, so he or she hits a lot of fat shots. Alternatively, at the bottom of this player's swing the clubhead will not touch the ground, so that the ball is either hit thin or topped while the clubhead is starting back up. But perhaps the most damaging problem this golfer has, like the one-planer who lacks shoulder rotation, is that this straight-line path of the club means that the clubface must be rotated from an extremely open position shortly before impact to an extremely closed clubface position right after impact. You can easily see this for yourself if you try to bring a club down and through the impact area on a path that's very much like a Ferris wheel, going down and up in front of you. You'll see that with this path, you must rotate your right forearm severely over your left forearm through the impact zone; if you didn't rotate the forearms, you could not finish the golf swing.

With the clubface moving from wide open to dead shut so quickly,

Photo 8.8 Two-plane correct body start but must now turn through to the finish

Photo 8.9 Two-plane fault of excessive arm release because of no body turn

it is extremely easy for the clubface to make contact while it's still open, or after it's closed. (As you can imagine, even a slight difference in the ball's position in the stance can also make a huge difference in where the clubface is pointing at impact for this player.) So both big slices and wild hooks can be the result of swings that appear to be identical. No wonder you never know what will happen on the next swing.

What do you do to alter this dangerous downswing path? There are several adjustments. First, try to reduce the magnitude of your hip slide. Think of it more as making just a bump to the left with your forward hip. As a checkpoint, you should feel as though your weight has shifted

Photo 8.10 Two-plane body rotation must continue through impact to the finish.

only slightly more onto your left foot; say 60 percent left, no more, immediately after making this lateral bump move. With this lessened hip slide, the hips should feel almost level throughout the downswing, rather than having the left hip tilted up.

Next, try to time your shoulder turn so it starts a bit earlier. It should come right after the left hip bump, either simultaneously with the arm drop or even a fraction before it. Your shoulder turn should be close to level, like the turning of a merry-go-round. Make sure that you rotate your entire upper torso as you turn through the shot.

Finally, ask a friend to make sure you are keeping your spine angle erect, never dipping during the downswing, and also that your spine tilt, when viewed from in front, is neutral or straight up-and-down, as opposed to tilting away from the target.

If you have not been turning enough on the downswing, two drills you should practice are the Club Across Shoulders Drill (Variation 4) and the Helicopter Drill, described in Chapter 9.

=========================== **Fact Versus Feel** ===========================

If you have been sliding too much laterally and not turning the body enough, it is in **fact** possible that you may overcorrect to the point where your swing path becomes a bit steep and from the outside-in. Should you notice this occurring, you can adjust in one of the following two ways: Delay the turning of your shoulders into the downswing just slightly, or tilt the spine slightly to the right on the downswing and keep your head a bit farther behind the ball.

That possibility aside, as you make the prescribed adjustments, it is likely that you will feel the following sensations: First, it will **feel** as if you are making more of a chest rotation than ever before (and hopefully, you are). The movement of your shoulders will **feel** very much like you are coming over the top of the shot. Last, at impact, it will **feel** like you are hitting down on the ball more and that you are swinging the club way to the left of your target through impact. Do not be alarmed by any of these sensations. If you pair the correct movement of your arms with the ideal body movements as described, you'll see immediate improvements in your power and accuracy.

157

Part Two: Model Two-Plane Downswing Arms and Club Positions and Movements

If you opt for the two-plane golf swing, you must supply a strong downward force with your arms on the downswing. As I have stated before, the two force planes that blend together to make a two-plane golf swing are the near-horizontal turning of the body combined with the vertical lifting and chopping motion of the arms.

As we discussed in the previous section, you will start the downswing by sliding the hips laterally toward the target. This move is coupled with the initial drop of your hands, arms, and the club down your right side, or away from the target. Next, your shoulders and hips turn through the downswing at the same pace as the arms continue to swing the club vertically downward.

As a two-plane golfer, remember that you must be aggressive with this downward chopping move. A good image, as you are swinging down, is that there is a wooden board propped up against the seam of your pants at your side just below your belt. You want to swing your arms down just as if you were planning to split that board in half with a karate chop.

While this chopping-down action is occurring, the turning of your shoulders will automatically bring your arms outward toward and through the impact zone. As they move, your right or rear forearm must cross over your left. This forearm rotation should bring the clubface from its relatively open position halfway through the downswing (toe pointing straight up with club shaft parallel to the ground behind you) to a closed position halfway into the follow-through (toe again pointing straight up with club shaft parallel to the ground in front of you). As a two-plane player, you must be conscious of this forearm rotation because, unlike the one-plane swing in which the movement

Photo 8.11 Two-plane downswing is a combination of hip slide/arm drop and then turning the body.

Photo 8.12 Two-plane right arm rotation over the left as the body turns through impact

of the arms and body on the inner circle squares the clubface to the target, your swing is dominated by the crossover of the arms. And since that movement is initiated by a downward chop (which does not by itself rotate the clubface), you need to actively rotate your right or rear forearm over your left or lead forearm through the impact zone.

Let's now dissect the most common arm and club flaws that I see two-plane golfers commit on their downswings and address them in the form of lessons as I do with my students.

LESSON: Curing a Faulty Inside-Out Arm Swing

Here we have a player with a timing problem: Either the arms start driving down sooner, or faster, than the body makes its turn; or alternatively, the body turn is too late or too slow for the driving of the arms. This golfer may be keeping his or her back turned to the target a little too long. This player usually has an ample lateral hip slide, but the shoulders are tilting more than they are turning as the arms are driving down. This player cannot help but swing the club into the ball from well inside the target line, on a shallow plane. Because of this, he or she is very prone to having the club catch the ground behind and slightly to the inside of the ball, resulting in a weakly hit shot that's often referred to as a "drop kick." Alternatively, this player may hit thin or topped shots. With the club coming from way inside the target line, this player tends to hit the ball off the toe, which usually results in an uncontrollable duck hook. Shots pushed to the right are a less-frequent but fairly common occurrence.

If you are struggling with this timing problem, you must work on delaying your hip slide and arm drop. Try to get your shoulders turning earlier, a split second before your hips slide and your arms drop. Try to make your shoulders turn levelly, along the same plane in which they were set in your address posture. Your hip turn should be as level as possible as well.

As your body rotates through impact, make your arms swing actively around to your left. With an iron club, you should take a divot that is not only in front of the ball, but also turning to the left, or inside the target line. Keep moving the handle of the club to the left until you are hitting fades.

Photo 8.13 Two-plane downswing fault of too much inside-out resulting in pushes and hooks.

Photo 8.14 Two-plane correction swinging club handle left with divot left and fade ball flight

The fade is the opposite ball flight of your ever-present hook. If you can find the opposite ball flight of your mistake, then you know the extent of the timing exaggeration you must feel. But until you can hit the left-to-right shot that starts to the left of your target line, you have not overdone anything.

If you are a two-planer who is swinging the club too much from the inside, three beneficial drills to work on are the Anti-Hook Grip Pressure Drill, the Club Across Shoulders Drill (Variation 4), and the Helicopter Drill, all described in Chapter 9.

Fact Versus Feel

As you work to speed up your body turn, in the downswing it will definitely **feel** as though your shoulders are turning too fast, and that your arms and the club are coming over the top. You may, in **fact**, make a correction to where, for a while at least, your body does turn faster than you drive down with your arms. If this occurs, your club's path down into the ball might actually get a little steeper than you'd like and also a bit outside-in; thus a fade or a slice might temporarily result. If so, there are two adjustments you can make: First, ratchet back the speed of your shoulder turn just a little, as it is now ahead of your downward arm drop. Alternatively, you can lighten the pressure from the base of your right thumb on top of your left thumb as you swing down. (This is, in effect, the opposite of the Anti-Hook Grip Pressure Drill.)

LESSON: Curing an Outside-In Arm Swing Problem

This timing problem occurs when the player is turning his or her upper torso faster than, or earlier than, the arms are dropping behind him or her. This problem will often happen when the player does not make the lateral sliding movement of the hips to start the downswing.

Because of this too-early shoulder turn in the two-plane swing, the player's arms and the club are thrown outside the correct plane early in the downswing. Once there, the club must come down to the ball steeply and from the outside-in. This player can hit fat pop-ups, pull-slices, and steeply topped shots.

Sometimes this player will also struggle with the straight-line impact we have talked about, in which he or she must try to rotate the clubface to square right at impact; either slices or hooks can be the result.

If these problems sound like yours, you need to make the following timing corrections: As your first downswing move, make your lateral hip slide toward the target, with the concurrent dropping of your arms behind you. After your hip slide, you should allow your right or rear shoulder to tilt down somewhat. Tilting the right shoulder down will accentuate your arm drop.

As you continue the downswing, you should feel as though you are delaying the turning of your shoulders until you reach impact. (In actuality, they will be turning well before that. But your key is to feel as though you are holding back your shoulder turn through most of the downswing.) Finally, try to swing your arms from inside the target line prior to impact, to across the target line just beyond impact.

161

Photo 8.15 Two-plane outside-in and steep downswing

Photo 8.16 Two-plane correction of lateral hip slide, spine tilt to the right, and lower right shoulder

Photo 8.17 Two-plane inside-to-out correction

Again, it is highly unlikely that your arms will ever get so far from your body as to get the clubhead outside the target line, but this is the movement you need to key on if you are a chronic outside-in, downward, chop-slice player.

If you are a two-plane swinger who is chopping across the ball from outside-in, practice the Hip Slide/Arm Drop Drill described in Chapter 9.

Fact Versus Feel

If you overcorrect to the point where your swing path actually does become very shallow and inside-out, and you begin hooking your shots, congratulate yourself for correcting your major problem. Now you just have to ratchet back your corrective measures slightly. It is a **fact** that you can find the happy medium, and hit straight shots, by simply allowing your shoulders to turn a little earlier than you have been—don't consciously hold back the shoulders. If you find after this adjustment that you are still drawing the ball some, you can also apply the principle of the Anti-Hook Grip Pressure Drill, that is, increase the pressure with the base of your right thumb onto your left thumb during the downswing.

That said, when you are trying to correct the outside-in arm swing, it will **feel** as though your arms are dropping way too far at the start of the downswing, or as though your forearms are way down near your pants leg. It will also **feel** as though you are reaching impact with your back still facing the target. Obviously, none of these sensations is actually happening, as you will see if you practice the timing of your downswing in front of a full-length mirror as you should.

LESSON: Sure Cure for Hitting a Mix of Hooks and Slice Shots

If you are a golfer who often hooks one shot and then slices the next, which is often referred to as "army golf," well, you've got a real problem. A golfer who struggles with one specific type of curve ball can sometimes play for it and manage his or her way around the course fairly effectively. But if you don't know what's coming next, there's no way you can consistently avoid trouble.

There's usually one simple reason a player might be prone to both slices and hooks: He or she stops turning the hips and upper torso through the impact zone. If you stop turning your hips and shoulders, the clubhead's path will usu-

Photo 8.18 Two-plane fault of stopping body rotation at impact and clubface held open too long

Photo 8.19 Two-plane fault of clubface held open too long and then flipping closed too rapidly

ally be on too much of a straight line through impact, with the clubface still very open as it nears impact.

From there it is, in my opinion, simply a matter of luck as to how the clubface meets the ball. If you don't flip the clubhead fast enough with your hands and forearms, the clubface will be open at impact and you'll slice the shot. If you happen to flip your forearms perfectly, the clubface will get squared up at just the right instant and you'll hit it straight. But if your forearm flip is too pronounced, you'll shut the clubface before impact and hit a low hook.

I don't like to single out PGA Tour professionals for their occasional flaws, because anyone who is out there is, by definition, a great player. But a notable example of this problem can sometimes be seen in the swing of one of the best players in the world, Phil Mickelson. At times when Phil is not at his best, he will slow down with his hips and upper body before impact. When that happens, he will instinctively make a very pronounced, rolling-over move of his left forearm over his right (since he is a left-handed golfer). And as great a player as he is, Mickelson is prone to wildness, especially with his driver, when he is swinging in this manner.

If two-time Masters champion Phil Mickelson can hit wild shots with this type of swing action, what are your chances of hitting accurate shots with it? I'd guess, just about zero. Your key should be to keep your hips and upper torso turning freely through and well beyond impact. If you keep your body turning, your arms and hands will not need to take over and try to salvage the shot. Yes, it is true that you will need to make some conscious forearm and club rotation in the two-plane downswing. However, this arm movement should never be made independent of turning your body. It may seem like I am asking you to pat your head and rub your stomach when I say to allow your right arm to roll over your left and continue to turn your body at the same time. But that is exactly what I am asking you to do, and I would not ask you if you couldn't do it. It just takes a little practice to keep moving your body while releasing your hands during impact.

Photos 8.20–8.21 Two-plane correction of turning body while releasing the club through impact

Practice the Two-Plane Release Drill (see Chapter 9) in front of a mirror to ingrain the correct forearm movement, then just keep turning while you do it.

Fact Versus Feel

It is a **fact** that too much arm release and too little body turn on the downswing can cause both hooking and slicing. (If the release is not fast enough, you'll push or slice; if the release is too fast, you'll hook.)

If you have been stopping your body before impact, when you keep both the body and the arms moving as they should you may **feel** like you are a baseball shortstop who, having fielded a slow grounder, is running and throwing at the same time. This is fine and to be expected as you swing correctly through the impact zone.

To sum things up, the two-plane downswing can be a very effective and powerful method of hitting the golf ball. It affords the less athletic or less flexible player a better chance to achieve distance on his or her shots because of the more active use of the arms and hands during the swing. However, the two-plane golfer will probably need more practice time in order to keep the body and the arms, hands, and club moving at the proper pace, while also moving on their proper respective planes. By practice, I mean working on drills, namely those contained in the following final chapter.

9

Two-Plane Drills

This chapter provides practice drills specifically designed to help you with the development of the two-plane golf swing. The drills are grouped according to the particular swing problems they help to correct. (Several drills that are beneficial to both one-plane and two-plane golfers are listed both here and in Chapter 5.)

I believe drills are vital in communicating the exact feels for making correct moves in the golf swing. Some drills are designed to give a better understanding of the entire swing. Other drills isolate a particular movement within the swing. Those isolated drills are not the entire swing but simply highlight a segment of the motion, and when learned, that segment is inserted back into the full swing. This is much like a mechanic who takes out a faulty engine, repairs it, and then reinstalls it. The isolated part is better repaired when removed from the whole and then replaced. Regardless of whether the drills are for isolated parts of the swing or for a full swing correction, try every drill that relates to each particular lesson that applies to your game. Your understanding of the correction you need to make will be greatly enhanced.

Photo 9.1 Club Across Shoulders Drill (Variation 4): Club shaft points beyond the zone

Fault: Reverse Pivot on Backswing

168

Club Across Shoulders Drill (Variation 4)

Hold a club across the front of your shoulders and assume your address posture for the two-plane swing. Turn your shoulders fully, on an angle that is bent forward 10 to 20 degrees from perfectly horizontal. Check that the club shaft (representing the turning angle of your shoulders) is pointing to the right of the ball and beyond, or outside of, the zone that runs from the ball to a spot on the ground 48 inches beyond it.

Repeat the drill, this time in front of a mirror, to check whether your

Photo 9.2 Club Across Shoulders Drill (Variation 4): Club shaft turns past the ball

head and spine have shifted slightly to the right and rear (away from the target). Return to address and repeat several times, keeping the shoulder turn close to horizontal and allowing the spine to tilt slightly to the right or rear.

Wallet Pocket Left Drill

Assume the two-plane address position. Have a friend stand behind you and hold a club horizontal to the ground at hip height, with the grip just lightly touching the outside edge of your left hip.

Make a full turn with your upper body. As you make this turn, your left wallet pocket should stay in contact with the shaft through the completion of the backswing.

As an alternate to having a friend hold a club, you can perform the drill by sticking a golf shaft in the ground so that it's standing vertically with the grip just touching your left hip. Make the same backswing movement so that your left wallet pocket stays in contact with the grip.

Photo 9.3 Wallet Pocket Left Drill: Club shaft just touching left hip at address

Photo 9.4 Wallet Pocket Left Drill: Left hip maintaining contact with the club shaft at top of backswing

Fault: Arms Too Far Outside/Narrow Backswing Arc

Turn and Face Club Drill

Set up as you normally would for a two-plane swing. Then practice making a start to the backswing in which you turn your shoulders and hips, along with the club, to a position where the club shaft is parallel to the ground halfway back.

When the club reaches this position, your torso should also have turned nearly 90 degrees, which is to say it is nearly facing the same way as the club shaft is pointing. Pause for a moment. Then complete the backswing (as well as the drill) from there by simply folding your arms and the club up to the top.

Repeat several times. This drill teaches you to increase the speed of the turning of your body in relation to the lifting of the club with your arms.

Photo 9.5 Turn and Face Club Drill: Turn and face the club at midpoint of backswing.

Photo 9.6 Turn and Face Club Drill: Complete the backswing by folding the club shaft up.

Fault: Arms Too Much Around/Too Inside on Backswing

Stand Near a Wall Drill

Take your address position with a five-iron, with your heels about 12 inches away from a wall (a tree will also suffice).

Now, execute the backswing in slow motion, taking the club back in such a manner that the clubhead never makes contact with the wall.

In order to do this, you'll need to begin lifting the club with your arms from the outset. If you start back with a turn of your hips and shoulders, you'll fling the club inside the target line and the clubhead will strike the wall well before you reach the top.

Keep repeating these slow-motion swings and feel the lifting with the arms necessary to keep the clubhead in front of the wall. When you are doing this successfully, you can adjust the drill slightly by moving your heels out to 15 inches away from the wall, which will allow you to turn the body a little more in conjunction with your arm lift.

Photo 9.7 Stand Near a Wall Drill: At address about a foot from a wall

Photo 9.8 Stand Near a Wall Drill: Swing to a correct top of backswing without hitting the wall.

Photo 9.9 Stand Near a Wall Drill: Incorrect arm and club movement will result in hitting the wall.

Fault: Too-Early Shoulder Turn on Downswing

Hip Slide/Arm Drop Drill

Take an iron club and swing it up to the top-of-backswing position. Hold the position for a second. Then, with your shoulders turned so that your back is more or less facing the target, slide your left or lead hip laterally toward your target. This lateral hip slide should be strong enough that your knees are also pulled laterally and your weight moves onto your left foot. As you make this lateral hip slide, let your arms, hands, and the club drop straight down. Your arms and the club should still be directly opposite your right side. However, your hands, which started at just above the level of your shoulders, should now be dropped to a point slightly above your waist. Your wrists should still be cocked so that the club shaft is still angled somewhat upward.

Repeat this move in front of a mirror until it automatically becomes the very first movement of your downswing when you're out on the course.

Photo 9.10 Hip Slide/Arm Drop Drill: Swing to a correct top-of-backswing position.

Photo 9.11 Hip Slide/Arm Drop Drill: With no body turn, slide the hips and drop the arms.

Fault: Lateral Slide and Tilt on Downswing

Club Across Shoulders Drill (Variation 5)

Set up for the two-plane swing while holding a club across the front of your shoulders. Make a full backswing turn and hold that position, so that the shoulders have turned at or near 90 degrees and the club shaft is pointing above the ball and to the outside of the zone.

From this position, turn your hips and shoulders fully until they are facing the target, with your weight fully on your left leg and your right foot resting on your toes.

The shoulder plane should point beyond the zone. This indicates that you are turning your shoulders on the correct, nearly horizontal plane for the two-plane swing. Repeat several times.

Photo 9.12 Club Across Shoulders Drill (Variation 5): Shoulder plane pointing beyond the zone

Photo 9.13 Club Across Shoulders Drill (Variation 5): Shoulder plane in follow-through points beyond the zone.

Helicopter Drill

Stand upright and spread your arms out wide away from you, parallel to the ground at shoulder height. While facing straight ahead, turn your shoulders horizontally as far as you can to your right. Then turn them back as far as you can to your left. Keep making this turning motion so your arms are like the rotors on a helicopter. As you turn, make sure to keep your arms parallel to the ground. If you notice one arm dipping while the other is rising, it means you're allowing your shoulders to tilt at the same time they are turning.

Photo 9.14 Helicopter Drill: Stand erect with arms extended perpendicular to the body and parallel to the ground.

Photo 9.15 Helicopter Drill: Keep the spine erect and the shoulders and arms parallel to the ground while turning in the backswing.

Photo 9.16 Helicopter Drill: Keep the spine erect and the shoulders and arms parallel to the ground while turning in the downswing.

Fault: Arms Swinging Inside-Out on Downswing

Anti-Hook Grip Pressure Drill

Find a very small object like a BB, a small pellet, a twig, or even a hard kernel of corn. Put your left hand on the grip, holding the club up so that the base of your left thumb is parallel to the ground. Place the small object just behind the second knuckle on your left thumb. Then carefully take your right hand grip so that the base of your right thumb covers the object and holds it in place.

Now take some practice swings. As you swing down through impact, increase the pressure with the base or heel of your right palm on the object, never allowing it to slip out. When you are consistently adding pressure and holding the object in place, you can try this drill on the practice range while hitting actual shots.

Club Across Shoulders Drill (Variation 5)

This drill is described on page 173.

Helicopter Drill

This drill is described on page 174.

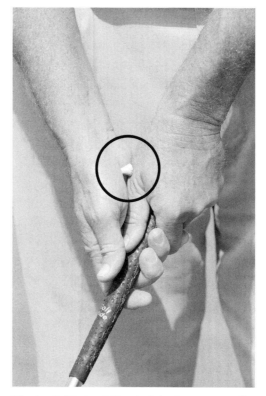

Photo 9.17 Anti-Hook Grip Pressure Drill: Squeeze an object between the right palm heel pad and the base of the left thumb.

Fault: Arms Swinging Outside-In on Downswing

Hip Slide/Arm Drop Drill

This drill is described on page 172.

Fault: Mixture of Hooks and Slices

Two-Plane Release Drill

This drill also appeared in *The Plane Truth for Golfers*, but it is well worth repeating. Assume your stance with a middle iron. Draw the club back to a point where the club shaft is parallel to the ground, at about hip height behind you. At this point, the toe of the club should point straight up. If it does not, rotate your forearms in the direction that will make the toe point straight up.

From this point, bring the club down to the point of impact. While doing so start to rotate your right or rear forearm in such a way that the clubface returns to face square to the target.

Pause at the point of impact to make sure the clubface is square. (Most two-plane golfers don't rotate the right forearm enough, so that the clubface would be left open at this point.)

Next, continue in slow motion to a point beyond impact where the club shaft is parallel to the ground with the clubhead in front of you. The toe of the club should again point straight up.

Photo 9.18 Two-Plane Release Drill: Club shaft is parallel to both the target line and the ground with the toe up.

Photo 9.19 *Two-Plane Release Drill:* Right arm rotates enough to bring the club back to square at impact.

Photo 9.20 Two-Plane Release Drill: Right arm continues to rotate over the left until the club shaft is parallel to both the target and the ground with the toe up.

If it points to the right, you need to rotate your right forearm more; if it points left, you need to rotate your forearm a little less through this point.

Practice this drill often, keeping it in slow motion, until you can automatically swing the club with the proper forearm rotation to make the clubface work from toe-up to toe-up on either side of the ball.

Index

About the Authors

Jim Hardy is a golf instructor par excellence. A former PGA tour professional, he is a teacher's teacher and a mentor to many of today's PGA Tour stars.

Among his students have been Frank Beard, Dave Stockton, Carol Mann, Donna Caponi, Hollis Stacy, Brad Faxon, Paul Azinger, and Mark O'Meara. He currently teaches PGA Tour professionals Peter Jacobsen, Scott McCarron, Tom Pernice, Bob Tway, Olin Browne, Duffy Waldorf, Jay Delsing, Stan Utley, Chris Tidland, Don Pooley, and Graham Marsh. Among the nationally recognized golf instructors who have studied under Jim are Hank Haney, Mike and Sandy LaBauve, Jim Murphy, Laird Small, Martin Hall, Roger Gunn, Paul Gorman, Chris O'Connell, Krista Dunton, Marty Fleckman, E. J. Pfister, Carol Mann, and Rick Sellers.

Jim's first book, *The Plane Truth for Golfers*, was America's bestselling golf instructional book of 2005. It was also nominated for USGA's 2005 Golf Book of the Year Award.

During his 40 years in professional golf, Jim Hardy has sought out experiences and opportunities that span the golf profession. His career in professional golf followed graduation from Oklahoma State University where he earned all-American honors in 1966. After an assistant professional position in Chicago and a head professional position on Cape Cod, Massachusetts, Jim passed the PGA Tour Q-School in 1968 and played the Tour full time until March 1974. From then through 1976 he served as head professional at Exmoor Country Club in Highland Park, Illinois.

In 1975, while instructing in Golf Digest Schools, Jim taught with England's John Jacobs and established an association with Jacobs that lead to *Golf Magazine*. Jim became a feature instructor with the Golf Magazine Schools and an instructional contributor for the magazine. Subsequently he cofounded, along with Shelby Futch, the John Jacobs Golf Schools and the Carol Mann Golf Schools and was the director of both enterprises.

In 1979 he left the golf schools and established his own instructional programs in Palm Springs, California, and Houston, Texas. Although he taught golfers of every level, he developed a strong clientele of professional golfers, top collegiate players, and golf teachers. In 1982 Jim limited his teaching to seminars, teaching professionals, and tour players while he expanded his career to include golf course design, golf course and club development, marketing, and operations. To date, he has either designed, developed, or operated more than 60 facilities.

Beyond his *Golf Magazine* credits, Jim has been a color analyst for golf network telecasts for NBC and ESPN. He was the featured instructor at the 1990 Teaching and Coaching Summit. His taped presentation from that summit is still one of the PGA's best-selling instructional tapes. In addition, he was a featured instructor at the 1994 and 2004 PGA International Teaching and Coaching Summit, and in 2000 he was the featured head instructor at the European Teaching and Coaching Summit. He has also taught at numerous local and sectional PGA seminars throughout the United States. In 1996, 2004, and 2006 he was named to *Golf Magazine*'s top 100 teachers. In 2001, 2003, and 2005 he was ranked in the top 50 by *Golf Digest* (and is currently ranked sixteenth). Jim received a nomination in 2001 and 2006 to the World Golf Hall of Fame Teacher's Division. In 2002 and in 2005 he was named the Harvey Penick Teacher of the Year by his PGA section.

John Andrisani, a native New Yorker, was assistant editor for Britain's popular weekly magazine, *Golf Illustrated*, and golf writer for *The Surrey County Magazine* (Surrey, England) before joining *Golf Magazine*. He was both senior editor of instruction and consulting editor for *Golf Magazine* from 1982–1998.

During his long stint at *Golf Magazine*, Andrisani's major focus was working with top teachers and tour pros to develop innovative and helpful instructional cover stories and feature articles. Andrisani has coauthored major instructional books with the game's top tour pros including the national bestseller *The Plane Truth for Golfers.*

Andrisani's popular instructional articles, travel pieces, humorous short stories, and interviews have also appeared in golfing and nongolfing publications worldwide, including *Playboy, Golf France,* and *Golf Germany* magazines. Additionally, he collaborated on a five-year instruction strip with Greg Norman for England's *Sunday Express* newspaper.

A former course record holder and winner of the World Golf Writers' Championship, Andrisani plays off a six handicap at the Pasadena Yacht and Country Club in Gulfport, Florida. Furthermore, he has played rounds with some of the world's greatest golfers, including former British Open and Masters champion Sandy Lyle, two-time U.S. Open winner Curtis Strange, multiple major championship winner Seve Ballesteros, and shot-making virtuoso Chi Chi Rodriguez.

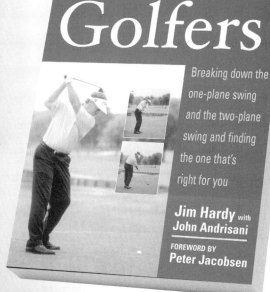